REBOOT

Becoming a Passionate
Follower of Jesus Christ

Justin R. Jones

ISBN: 1983669865
ISBN-13: 978-1983669866

To my Grandparents:
Who set the tone in my family for living as passionate
followers of Jesus Christ.

To my Son:
Who I hope reads this one day and lives it out more
passionately than I ever could!

To my Lord and Savior Jesus Christ:
This book is about Him, for Him, and to Him!

ACKNOWLEDGMENTS

A big thank you to:

- Shawn King for his help in discerning some of the themes for the book
- Janelle Jones, C. Ray Miller, Dawn Waggoner, Joni Canastraro, Corey Nieman, and others who helped get the book ready for publishing
- My Spiritual Formation teams for their feedback and insights
- The people of Eastern Hills Church for their love and support

CONTENTS

Acknowledgments   i

1 Introduction   1

2 **Technology Graveyard**: Rebooting the Power of   9
   our Spiritual Life

3 **Fundamental Promises**: Rebooting the Promises of   31
   our Spiritual Life

4 **Effectively Ineffective**: Rebooting the Practices of 53
   our Spiritual Life

5 **Mental Volatility**: Rebooting the Memory of our   83
   Spiritual Life

6 **Firewall Free Fall**: Rebooting Discernment in our   105
   Spiritual Life

7 **Fatal Fragmentation**: Rebooting Urgency in our   135
   Spiritual Life

8 Conclusion   165

   Notes   170

INTRODUCTION

When I was a teenager I had an old Mac laptop. It was a good and reliable computer for several years until the screen started to fade. While I was working on it I would have to strain my eyes to see anything. I am not the most technologically savvy person, but I decided that instead of paying someone to fix this problem I would do it myself. I searched online, diagnosed the problem, talked to my dad, and we devised a plan. The piece we needed to replace was easy to buy and seemingly easy to install, but unfortunately, we had to take the whole computer apart to get to the screen. We read some online directions and with great optimism we set up an impromptu computer lab at our dining room table.

We started to take the computer apart piece by piece, starting with the larger elements like the battery and case and then the smaller instruments inside that had tiny little screws. We were completely focused and had organized a system of bags that we put each section of pieces into so we did not lose anything. We worked for hours and hours. After replacing the part that was broken, we slowly put everything back together

1

and the moment of truth finally came. We were both excited, but neither one of us really wanted to push the button. One of us was going to have to test it – would the computer boot up again?

I pushed the button and suddenly there was a bright splash of blue across the screen. My confidence soared and I was about to start congratulating us when an awful sound screamed out from the computer. It was a crunchy, crackling noise that was somewhat reminiscent of the old dial-up modems in the early days of the internet. This was not a happy crackling noise though. It was the kind of noise where you knew something was breaking and there was nothing you could do about it. The computer was completely ruined.

Our best guess was that something we had done had destroyed the motherboard. There was no recovering this computer on our own. Unless we enlisted the help of an expert, it was at best a paperweight. At worst, it was destined for the recycling pile. I was so sad and frustrated. I had put so much hope into the belief that I could fix my computer's problems and in the end my best efforts led to nothing.

As I have watched the lives of people over my lifetime and think back over the many conversations I have had with people within our church, I believe this is a common feeling most people have about their faith. At some point in their life, they noticed something was broken within them, and recognized something needed to be done. They were told about the Gospel and started a relationship with Jesus, but beyond that they did not have much clarity.

They heard great statements about what their life could look like and initially got excited. For instance, maybe they heard a mission statement like our church has, "Engaging every person to become a passionate follower of Jesus Christ."

The idea of becoming someone different than they were before and living a bold and passionate life sounded great. Who does not want to leave behind the broken parts of life for a passionate, fulfilled life?

The problem is many of us hear these statements and have no idea how to truly live them out. Not knowing what to do, we often take the same risk I took with the computer. We start trying to fix our own lives. We put a lot of effort into it, taking the pieces of our lives apart and dealing with them each individually. We try to carefully place everything where we think it needs to go. We "replace" pieces of our life that we think need to change. We try to "rewire" certain thoughts and feelings in our life. We look for advice and try to carefully follow that advice.

Unfortunately, after all that hard work, our lives do not look much different than they did before. We have the same problems we always struggle with. We do not feel passionate. In fact, for some of us, our lives seem to fall apart more than they did before. Maybe after all of this, some of us start to doubt if following Jesus is worth it. What does our faith in Jesus mean if it doesn't change us?

Most of us do not fully walk away from Jesus, but we hold onto a lot of unanswered questions. We push our feelings down deep inside of us. Instead of our feelings and actions aligning, we start to do things out of obligation. We may still try to live "good" lives, but we also start to run to other things that make us feel good in the moment.

Thus begins the most common and yet rarely understood disease of modern American Christianity: apathy. Apathy is defined as "absence or suppression of passion, emotion, or excitement."[1] It pervades almost every element of modern Christian families and churches, and yet we do not seem to think it is a serious problem.

Ministry leaders complain about apathetic churches like they might complain about weeds in a garden: "It's terrible, but what are you going to do? It's a fact of life." Parents talk about apathetic children like it's a normal state of spiritual growth: "You know, they run away for a little while and sow their wild oats, but they will come back again." Older Christians sometimes even wear their apathy like a badge of honor: "Oh, that's so cute how passionate those young believers are. I remember those days. They will come down off that mountain of emotion sometime soon and find out not everything turns out the way they hope it will."

Unfortunately, these responses do nothing to stem the tide of broken lives, broken relationships, and a broken world. Apathetic churches continue as a broken and sometimes disgusting distortion of who God is, apathetic children end up not coming back to God as they get older, and those apathetic old Christians fall into a pharisaical, closed-off, grumpy lifestyle that does nothing to push the Kingdom of God forward.

Apathy in our faith is something we must not ignore. There is not a single verse in the New Testament that makes apathy sound normal. Jesus said He came "that they may have life, and have it to the full."[2] The early Christian church in the book of Acts is full of power and life. Miracles abounded, brokenness was defeated, and the church reflected something different than the world had ever seen – a group of people who were completely "one in heart and mind" and who stood "with great power" in life and speech about the resurrection of Jesus Christ.[3] Paul's letters attack all elements of apathy, calling for us to understand and embrace the transformed and passionate life God has planned for us.

There is one New Testament letter in particular I believe

speaks to this issue of apathy in a direct and yet gentle way: 2 Peter. This letter was not written by Paul, but instead was written by the apostle Peter toward the end of his life. In this letter, he speaks to the Christians of Western Asia Minor.[4] This is a group of people who lived in a world of persecution. They were a minority in the pagan culture of the day, with political and cultural forces aligned against them; not so different than the world we live in today.

Almost every part of our society today has become thoroughly pagan, or disassociated from the person of Jesus Christ. Our political, educational, and cultural systems are often in direct contrast to the ways of Jesus. Many university professors consider it their mission to completely eradicate any idea of God from the minds of unsuspecting college students. The entertainment and music industries are propelling anti-God worldviews into the minds of undiscerning people daily. Movies and TV shows peddle lies about God and ourselves into our minds, hidden behind comedy or drama that distracts us from the reality of what is really being said. Our justice, money, and even food systems are broken and disjointed, exposing the corruption and greed that lie behind.

Unfortunately, this pressure is not just from outside the church. Many churches have hidden scandals, infighting, and "politics." Among many spiritual leaders there is a thirst for power more than passion for Jesus Christ. Disruptive people and destructive beliefs infiltrate many churches, confusing people about what is true. The atmosphere surrounding us is ripe for apathy.

Peter is speaking to an audience in 2 Peter that is experiencing a similar atmosphere. He desperately wants the church to understand that apathy is not the only option. In the letter, he offers clear guidelines for how to become and remain a passionate follower of Jesus Christ. These guidelines do not involve trying to "fix yourself" which is how we so often try to do it. Instead, he wants them (and us) to see the great power of God we have access to and how that power helps us to live a passionate and fulfilled life. He does all of this while speaking with a shepherd's heart.

In this book, I would like to take what Peter says in 2 Peter and use it as a foundation for us to know what it means to break free from apathy and become a passionate follower of Jesus Christ. I hope to be direct and clear in confronting apathy, while also speaking with a shepherd's heart like Peter, understanding heart issues can be difficult to confront.

I've called this book "Reboot" because I will use the illustration of a computer as a backdrop to explore the inner workings of apathy and how God says to break free from it. According to Merriam Webster Dictionary "reboot" means "to shut down and restart (a computer or program)" or "to start (something) anew: to refresh (something) by making a new start or creating a new version."[5] Technology can be a fickle thing and many times computers need a reboot.

Maybe you get a brand-new computer and need to install some software. Maybe your computer has just been working hard for a long time and needs a quick reboot to get back on track. Maybe there is a virus or systemic problem in the computer and you need to reboot in order to fix it. Or maybe you get the dreaded "blue screen of death" and there is no option but to reboot. Whatever the case, computers often need a reboot.

In the same way, maybe you are new to this whole "Jesus thing" and you need a reboot to "install new programs" so you do not start your faith journey off in a wrong direction. Maybe you have been a Christian for a long time and you need a quick reboot in your faith to get it back in working order. Maybe you are dealing with some serious questions in your life or walking through a really difficult time of divorce, grief, addiction, or something else and it feels like you have no option but to reboot. Whatever the case, this book is for you.

As we begin, please understand that apathy is something that inherently does not want to be confronted. There is a good chance you might begin this journey and then try to run away from it as soon as it feels uncomfortable. I encourage you to share this journey with someone: a family member, a friend, a small group, or a mentor. Agree before you begin that you will hold each other accountable to not only listen to the words being said, but also act on them. James 1:22-25 says this:

> *Do not merely listen to the word, and so deceive yourselves. Do what it says. Anyone who listens to the word but does not do what it says is like a man who looks at his face in a mirror and, after looking at himself, goes away and immediately forgets what he looks like. But the man who looks intently into the perfect law that gives freedom, and continues to do this, not forgetting what he has heard, but doing it – he will be blessed in what he does.*

My hope is to put forth plainly what God says through 2 Peter about our spiritual growth. As we hear what He says to us, we must remember that action is a necessary next step. Take a second and pray that God would open your eyes to what He desires for you as you continue reading.

REBOOT

Chapter 1

Technology Graveyard
REBOOTING THE POWER OF OUR SPIRITUAL LIFE

I was cleaning out our garage recently, and I came across a box that held what I like to term my "technology graveyard." It is the final resting place of my old, outdated, and broken technology including computers, phones, and other things. I hold on to them because of this fanciful idea that I will someday use their parts to fix something else, but it never works that way. They just sit there, collecting dust, becoming more and more of a relic the longer they age.

Honestly, I think part of the reason I let them sit there instead of getting rid of them is because I feel bad. For some of the technology, it was functioning fine and normal, but I upgraded to something else. The hardware became out of date and unable to handle the stress of new updates. It is not that it was a bad computer or phone or tablet. It just could not handle the stress.

Even worse are the pieces of technology that are completely fine, but their hardware is broken and unusable. For instance, one year for Christmas I got this electronic guitar machine. It was like an electric guitar, but it also had computer synth sounds and other features you could use with it. I love playing instruments and this was an exciting gift to me. Unfortunately, when I plugged it in I used the wrong kind of cord. It destroyed the hardware of the guitar and it was completely unusable after that.

So it is with many pieces of technology in my "technology graveyard." Because their hardware is broken, their usefulness for the purpose they were designed is completely gone. The term "hardware" is defined as "the machines, wiring, and other physical components of a computer or other electronic system."[6] These are the essential physical pieces of a computer or piece of technology.

The other major part of a computer or computing device is software. Software is "organized information in the form of operating systems, utilities, programs, and applications that enable computers to work."[7] Programmers encode information allowing the computer to do the things we take for granted every day.

There are many differences between hardware and software. Hardware is something built into the computer or piece of technology and is usually difficult for the average person to update. Software is updated all the time. You might have that annoying pop-up appear regularly on your computer asking you to update some part of the software.

Problems with the computer's software do not usually destroy the computer's ability to function, and even if they do you can usually just reinstall the software. If something in the hardware breaks or is badly out of date, though, it can completely destroy the ability of the computer to function. Usually only an expert can fix it.

The reason I bring up my "technology graveyard" and the broken hardware many of those computers have is because I think it is a good starting point for the discussion of apathy in our spiritual lives. I believe we have a misunderstanding of the actual source of apathy. For many of us, apathy can go unnoticed in our lives for a long period of time. We go about our business every day with the same routine: eating, planning, working, meeting, talking, relaxing, playing, and sleeping. Life may seem much more chaotic than a "routine" is supposed to feel, but the same elements are always part of life.

The only time apathy becomes apparent is when we come up against a road block. We might see a relationship start to decline, an addiction start to take hold, money start to become tight, or physical health start to decline in some way. We recognize something is wrong and if it is bad enough, we start to do something to correct it. Generally, this means we try to replace poor practices or actions with better ones.

We might try to fix our relationship by buying our spouse a gift or throw away the things related to an addiction or cut up a credit card or sign up for a gym or go on a diet. We feel good about ourselves and may even continue some of these practices for a while. Unfortunately, if we are to be honest, this does not solve the actual problem. Most of us simply fall back into bad patterns and practices after a little while. And others, who do continue with changed practices, find their sense of apathy simply becomes applied to something else in life. The reason this happens is because we have only dealt with the symptoms of apathy, not the actual source.

The source of apathy is so much deeper than just our practices. You see, our thoughts, feelings, and actions are like the "software" of our lives. These are very important and we are going to look at these aspects of our life within this book. But the reason we often find little progress in fighting against apathy in our lives is because we have not truly dealt with the source of apathy or the "hardware" issue. In 2 Peter, this is the first issue the apostle Peter tackles as he tries to encourage the Christians of his time. Ultimately, it has to do with our understanding of what powers us.

THE QUESTION OF POWER

How often do you think of what powers the things around you? Unless you have an engineering or mechanical mind, most people do not care about where things get power unless that power goes out. For instance, you might not care too much about what powers your house until you lose power in the middle of a storm. Or you might not care too much about the inner workings of an engine until your car stops working.

Even if we do not normally think about it, though, the simple but strangely important reality is that everything is powered by something. Whether it is as big as the fusion powering the sun or the daily food and water feeding our bodies, everything is powered by something.[8] And the potential of something is only limited by its ability to receive and process that power.

So, what powers your life? I'm not talking about the physical food and water this time. I mean what powers your everyday thoughts, feelings, and actions? Maybe you have never thought about it, but it is one of the most important questions you can ask yourself.

For most of us, the assumption would be ourselves. We

are in control of our lives, and we are the only ones that can ultimately change our thoughts, feelings and actions. But let me ask you: can you think of a single other creature or entity that can power itself and needs nothing outside of itself? Everything needs an outside power source. Every creature or entity is dependent on something else for survival. So why would we think our daily lives are any different?

Yet, we attempt to live this way on a regular basis with varying degrees of success. As I see it, we can have three different results when we attempt to live our lives in our own strength: success, failure, or intentional rebellion. All of them result in apathy, or a lack of passion.

The first one is relatively obvious. When we control our lives through intentional rebellion against God, the result will be less excitement and passion about God. When we know the Truth of how God says to live life and we intentionally choose to go against His way of living, we are deciding our way is better. We think that by controlling our lives we will discover some kind of pleasure, excitement, or satisfaction that God will not give us. This has been the clear deception of sin since the beginning of time. Unfortunately, this line of thinking is always wrong. We ultimately discover the lack of pleasure, excitement, or satisfaction in the path we have chosen.

This is the story of the Prodigal Son in Luke 15. The son decided that life apart from his father was going to bring about the pleasure and excitement he thought he could not find while living under his father's authority. So, he takes his inheritance and squanders his wealth on things the father would not support. Instead of finding great pleasure and excitement, he is left alone and penniless in a pen of pigs. His intentional rebellion against the ways of his father brought about pain. The same is true for us when we intentionally rebel against the ways of God. It only brings about pain and apathy.

For others, they are not living life in their own power out of an intentional rebellion. Instead, they simply think this is how God expects them to live. Maybe it was the denomination they grew up in, the family conversations they had, or some other form of teaching they listened to at some point. Whatever the case, they view God as the one who sets forth rules and laws for us to follow, but who does nothing to help us live out those rules and laws. All of the responsibility for living a godly life lands on us. God becomes someone reminiscent of a drill sergeant who hands us a very heavy backpack and tells us to run. We may even feel like He watches us as we struggle, waiting for us to fail so He can yell at us and tell us to get up and do it again.

There is a relatively small group of people that seem to thrive on this constant pressure to live up to God's rules and laws. They are always trying to jump higher and do better and seem to succeed at living up to these expectations most of the time. What they do not tell people around them is that despite the outward signs of success, there is a deep lack of peace inside of them. They may not even be aware of this lack of peace in themselves until they achieve the height of what they deem to be success in life and do not find the satisfaction they anticipated.

Most others who view God as a drill sergeant find they carry a constant sense of failure. They are working hard to do what they believe God has called them to do, but they are not as successful, not as righteous, not as kind, not as ... you can fill in the blank ... as they need to be. The more failure occurs, the more apathy grows. They are living their life under their own control and it is not working. Out of a constant sense of guilt or because they think God is not fair, they try to blame someone or something else for their failure like parents, teachers, friends, socioeconomic restraints, cultural pressures, and many other things. But deep down I think most people recognize that if they are living their life under their own power and control they have no one to blame but themselves if things go wrong.

Thus, we come to the source of apathy or lack of passion in our spiritual lives: depending on our own power as the source of our potential. Whether we rebel, succeed, or fail we are using ourselves as the benchmark. And whether we know it or not, when we do this we are practically eliminating the power of God from our daily lives. God is more of an idea to us, rather than a relationship that should change our whole being.

I was confronted with a similar version of this problem in regard to marriage. For most of my life, my "future wife" was an idea to me. I dreamed about what she might be like and I imagined what life might be like with her, but she was not present with me yet. Then I met my wife Janelle. She is an amazing woman and I have been so blessed by her, but what is so interesting is you can have all kinds of ideas about someone without having to actually confront who they are. What I mean is this: I might have had expectations about what marriage was going to be like, but I never had to put those expectations to the test because my "future wife" was not yet present in my life. When I actually got married to my beautiful wife, it was more amazing than I could have imagined, but it also changed me. You see, I could control the idea of my "future wife" and make her anything I wanted. But when I got married I had to deal with the reality of a relationship, not the idea of marriage.

In a similar way, I think most Christians are stuck in a place where God is mostly an idea. He is a subject to be studied or a set of rules to be followed. We go to church and sit through worship services, classes, and other events to study this idea we believe in, while not really feeling that there is much power in this faith we ascribe to. Or we have an idea of who God is, like the drill sergeant picture, but it is not a true idea. Whatever the case, we can control an idea, but we cannot control a person. When we control God like an idea, we put Him into a box and by doing so, we eliminate any power outside of our own understanding.

No wonder so many peoples' spiritual lives seem so anemic and apathetic. Depending on God as an idea might last us a little while, but it ultimately leaves us feeling empty and powerless. It is like a laptop running on battery power. It might keep going for a little while, but ultimately it will need to be plugged into a real power source.

HIS DIVINE POWER

Peter's words in 2 Peter 1 confront this power struggle directly. He says in 2 Peter 1:3, "His divine power has given us everything we need for a godly life through our knowledge of him who called us by his own glory and goodness." Think about that verse for a second. Read it over again. Before he ever encourages the Christians of that day to keep growing in their faith and before he tries to explain how to deal with difficult situations, he reminds them of the simple truth that it doesn't start with them. It is only by "His divine power" that they can do anything.

Let's break this down into its component parts and ask ourselves if we really believe it. First, do you really believe God has power? If you have been a follower of Christ for a long time this might seem like a strange question. Yet, remember how we talked about the fact that we often put God's power in a box? I find so often that people can talk a lot about God's power without really believing it to be true. A friend of mine went skydiving and sent me a video of his experience. As I watched it, I wondered to myself whether I would ever go skydiving? I do not have any qualms that the equipment, the airplane, and the person working there are not powerful enough to get me through the experience. I could probably even find some scientific information about the rarity of skydiving accidents and the many safety checks skydivers have to do in order to be prepared for a jump. Yet, for many years I have enjoyed an anonymous quote I discovered in college, "If at first you don't succeed, then skydiving is definitely not for you." At the end of the day, I am quite sure skydiving is safe, yet I am not sure I would ever put it to the test. In a similar way, I think people might "believe" God has power, but they are not willing to truly put it to the test.

So, what does the Bible really say about God's power? In Genesis He creates the universe out of nothing. In the several books following Genesis, He miraculously frees the Israelites from the rule of the political and military superpower of the day. In the rest of the Old Testament there are many displays of God's power and beautiful descriptions of His might in the poetry and prophecy books.

Then, in the New Testament the greatest demonstration of His power occurs in raising Jesus Christ from the dead. Many of the New Testament writers try to describe the unfathomable depths of God's power. Paul does this well in Ephesians 1:18-21:

> *I pray that the eyes of your heart may be enlightened in order that you may know the hope to which he has called you, the riches of his*

glorious inheritance in his holy people, and his incomparably great power for us who believe. That power is the same as the mighty strength he exerted when he raised Christ from the dead and seated him at his right hand in the heavenly realms, far above all rule and authority, power and dominion, and every name that is invoked, not only in the present age but also in the one to come.

Paul describes it as "his incomparably great power." Basically, He is so powerful that it would be almost comical to compare His power to other sources of power we understand.

Think of a nuclear bomb, one of the most powerful things man has attempted to harness. The nuclear bomb of today is 3000 times more powerful than the bombs dropped on Hiroshima and Nagasaki.[9] One of the atomic bombs we dropped, nicknamed "Little Boy," released the energy equivalent of 15,000 tons of TNT and had a mushroom cloud 25,000 feet high. The Tsar Bomba, the biggest bomb ever dropped, was far more powerful. In 1961, when the Soviet Union set off this bomb, it produced a blast equivalent to 50,000,000 tons of TNT. The mushroom cloud was 130,000 feet high. This is gargantuan power.

Yet, compare it to God's power. Do you realize God's power is so unfathomable that the power of a nuclear bomb would seem like a little spark? His power is limitless. He can create at will, out of nothing. He can bring dead things to life. There is no power of evil and darkness that can even remotely challenge Him. Great fear and awesome wonder accompany any story in Scripture where someone sees even a glimpse of the power and glory of God.

Now, despite everything I've just said, let's go back to the original question: do you believe God has power? I could talk all day long about how awesomely powerful God is, but if you still are not willing to believe His power is real you will never experience it. Paul was confident that God's incomparable power "belongs to men and women on this simple condition of their believing, that is, their laying hold of it, accepting it from him, as a gift that he wants them to have."[10] If you believe God has power, it will directly confront the source of apathy in our lives because all of a sudden we will have to consider that there is another source of power we have access to other than our own.

EVERYTHING WE NEED

Now, you might believe God has amazingly great power, but still ask how it applies to daily life? This is probably similar to what the Christians of Peter's time were thinking, "Is the power of Jesus Christ sufficient on its own to strengthen the resolve of anxious and tempted Christians in a tough and attractively pagan world?"[11] Even if we believe in God's power, does that power really apply to seemingly inconsequential activities of my daily life? Is God's power applicable every moment of every day or just in the big moments?

Peter responds with a clear statement, "His divine power has given us *everything we need.*" He does not give much room for flexibility. Peter says there is nothing we come in contact with and no scenario that can be imagined where God's power does not provide *everything we need.* Homrighausen remarks, "All that a person really wants for life and of life God has granted to men by his divine, self-generated power."[12]

Do you realize what this means? So many of us are tired. We are constantly searching for the missing ingredient in our lives to reach our ultimate potential. For those of us who have a relationship with Jesus, we know this relationship is a major part of our potential, but there is always part of us that thinks we need an additional element for everything to really come together. We are not satisfied with the simple truth that a relationship with Jesus provides all the power we need, and we go searching for the next sermon, the next speaker, the next book that will ultimately help us reach our potential. Lucas and Green put it this way:

> There will always be people who want to supplement the work of Christ with extra teaching, and convince us that we are living less than Christian lives, while their particular form of teaching is the ingredient missing from traditional Christianity. It takes different forms: Christ plus healing, Christ plus success, Christ plus prosperity, Christ plus counselling, Christ plus an overwhelming experience. Anxious Christians may spend many years going through these, searching for an assurance that is already theirs in Christ. Simply by being Christians we have access to everything we need to live a life that pleases God. Those who want to add to that are false teachers.[13]

Think of what it would be like to stop searching for the answer and simply live out the answer. What if you could get off the constant roller coaster of finding the "next big thing" and instead invest your energy into the true source of power? Whether you recognize it or not, when we are constantly on the search for the "missing ingredient" to our life, we are still living with ourselves as the source of our power. We believe that if we can find that one special thing and then take control of it, everything will finally come together. It is the draw of any infomercial or advertisement, "Buy this product and all of your problems will be solved." But when you finally get that product in the mail, it disappoints like all the previous ones did.

When we turn away from the simple reality that God's power is real and provides everything we need, "The result will be a consumer-orientated church suitable for a consumer-orientated society – and in the end, bitter disillusionment – but not before wave succeeds wave of 'special offers' and yet more exaggerated promises, each in turn to be laid aside in hopeless disappointment."[14] God's heart yearns for us to stop running to other things to find our potential and recognize He can provide everything we need.

HOW TO DO THIS?

You may recognize God's power is real and might be ready to consider that God's power is truly all we need, but how do we do this? The answer is pretty simple. Peter says in 2 Peter 1:3b that this divine power we have access to comes "through our knowledge of him who called us by his own glory and goodness." Peter uses two different words in Greek to talk about knowledge. One word is "gnosis" which is used in relation to knowing information. The other word for knowledge, "Epignosis," which is used in this passage, is different. Lucas and Green describe this word as having "the sense of 'personal knowledge,' the knowledge of a husband or wife or good friend that goes beyond knowing things *about* them and actually knows *them*."[15] So, Peter's solution to the source of apathy is to become real about God.

What do I mean by "becoming real" about God? Remember what the source of apathy is: depending on our own power as the source of our potential. In this chapter we've discussed how depending on our own power causes us to create an idea of God rather than knowing Him for real. This belief causes us to put God in a box, limiting His influence in our lives. As a result, we are constantly searching for that missing ingredient to supplement God's work in our lives. The problem with all of this is that it is not real.

It is like we are living out the movie "The Matrix." In the movie, Neo is living a normal life in a futuristic world when he is confronted by a man named Morpheus. Morpheus calls into question many of the things that Neo believes about the reality around him. Morpheus alludes to the fact that instead of the world being real, it is actually a complex computer program made to look real. Finally, Morpheus calls him to a point of a decision: does Neo really want to acknowledge the reality around him or keep living a fake life? In one scene, Morpheus gives Neo the choice of a red pill or blue pill. He says, "This is your last chance. After this, there is no turning back. You take the blue pill—the story ends, you wake up in your bed and believe whatever you want to believe. You take the red pill—you stay in Wonderland, and I show you how deep the rabbit hole goes. Remember: all I'm offering is the truth. Nothing more."[16]

Just like Morpheus called Neo to a point of decision, God, out of His own glory and goodness, calls to us. He offers us a chance to break free from the fake and apathetic reality many of us ascribe to. The only way we can break free from this is to truly know God, not just know about God. To do this, we must become real about ourselves, become real about God's power, and become real about the process.

BECOME REAL ABOUT OURSELVES

Remember how I talked about my "technology graveyard" at the beginning of the chapter? For most of the technology in that pile, there is something wrong with the "hardware" or the physical components of the device. Instead of being useful and powerful, these devices just sit there because I do not have the ability to fix the hardware of any of them. However, I have some friends that probably could repair them. These are people that are skilled and equipped to deal with the physical components of technology.

Now imagine we are those devices, sitting in my "technology graveyard." If we refused to acknowledge that the essential components within us were broken and in need of repair, what would happen to us? We would just sit there, not capable of living up to the potential we were created for. The reason we are constantly stuck in apathy is because we continually believe either that we are not broken or that we can fix ourselves.

We must become real about ourselves. We are created beings similar to how those pieces of technology were created by someone. Sin, like a virus, has invaded our "hardware" and destroyed our capacity to live according to the way God has designed us. From the very beginning, the temptation of sin has been depending on our own strength instead of depending on the power of God.

The Bible teaches us that we become real about ourselves through confession. Confession in a biblical context means "'to say the same thing' or 'to agree to a statement.'"[17] Becoming real about ourselves means to agree with God about our situation. You cannot find healing unless you are willing to acknowledge a sickness. In the same way, if we truly want to break free from apathy in our spiritual lives, it always begins with confession or becoming real about ourselves. Simply acknowledge to God that your "hardware" is broken and in need of repair. He is the only one capable of dealing with the "hardware" of your life. He is the one who created you. He is the only one who can fix you.

BECOME REAL ABOUT GOD

When I was in college I was on staff in the freshman guy's dorm for a couple of years. My resident director would take his staff on retreats occasionally and on one of those retreats we travelled to the Smokey Mountains. While there, I decided to take a walk and my RD came with me. Now, I am a pretty average person from a physical perspective, not exceptionally tall or big or strong. My RD, on the other hand, was a very tall and large man. He had a teddy bear personality, but if he wanted to he had the power to fight anyone.

We started out on the walk and were having a good time, when suddenly I heard a noise and realized we were being followed by a bear. I had never seen a wild bear up that close. It was a small bear, but if it wanted to it could still do a lot of damage to us. Faced with this challenge on my own, I would have darted and hoped for the best. But knowing I was standing there with my RD gave me some solace. To be perfectly honest, I knew if the bear attacked us it would probably have gone after him first, but beyond that I trusted his ability to confront the bear over my own.

How would it change your life if you knew for a fact you had God walking next to you every moment of every day? Not your limited idea of who God is, but the great and awesome God of the Bible. The God you cannot control, put into a box, or completely and fully understand. The God who "gives life to the dead and calls into being things that were not."[18] There is nothing that could stand in His way, nothing that would ever make Him hurry, and nothing that could resist His control. Everything He would come in contact with would have no choice but to bow down in reverence to His glory and goodness.

If we were to truly become real about God and the divine power He has provided to those who believe in him, our whole perspective on life would change. Think of the small and petty concerns we carry around on a daily basis about money, time, prestige, ability, relationships, popularity, etc. When we become real about God and His divine power, all of these things seem to shrink. We are no longer considering how our power stacks up against each one of these concerns, but how God's power stacks up against each one.

One of the easiest ways to become real about God's power is to again confess, but this confession is a little different. Instead of confessing our brokenness, we are confessing His greatness. What if our first reaction in every situation was to confess God's greatness over it? Our job might be stressful, but God is greater than any stress. Society might look completely broken, but God stands above any power or principality on the earth. Your marriage might be struggling, but God's power is greater than any brokenness within a marriage. Confessing God's greatness reminds us that His power is sufficient, no matter the circumstance.

BECOME REAL ABOUT THE PROCESS

Some of you may be really excited because in the last couple of paragraphs I finally got to the part of the chapter where I tell you what to do. If you follow your normal pattern, you will now take this information and try to practice it the best that you can. I told you to become real about yourself and real about God. You will go away from reading this and will work as hard as you can to be the best confessor of sin and

God's greatness that has ever existed. You will do all of this, not realizing you have missed out on the whole point. You see, you will have taken the information you received and simply continue to live life in your own power and control.

You can always control ideas and information like we said earlier, but no matter how hard you try you cannot control a relationship. Relationships are not static, one-time decisions. Relationships are a journey. Imagine if someone simply said their marriage vows and believed they had achieved the perfect marriage in that moment. The marriage vows are simply the confession and reminder of the commitment. The real work is the process of working those vows out in every part of daily life. This is a process and a journey that never ends if you want a healthy and growing marriage.

The same can be said about our relationship with God. If you think you can simply confess a couple things to God and in so doing break free from apathy, then you must become real about the process. The process is where you actually experience the power of God in everyday life. It is constantly bringing the "hardware" of your heart before God on a daily basis and again asking Him to do His work.

It is confessing God's greatness the minute anxiety overtakes your mind. It is confessing your brokenness to God and to your spouse immediately after you have a fight. It is asking God to expand your understanding of how powerful He is. It is taking steps of faith that will push yourself into the arms of God instead of the arms of false comfort. We will spend the rest of the book talking more about how to do all of this, but it starts with simply becoming real about the process.

The picture I keep in mind to remind me of this process is the picture of cutting an onion. We picked some onions from our garden this summer and they were extremely pungent. When I would cut them, immediately tears would well up in my eyes and I would try to rub them because of the pain. I would stop for a second and then go back to cutting. The onions would always taste great in the dishes we made, but we had to be willing to go through the tears and pain that came along with cutting the onions in order to enjoy them in the meal.

I think this is similar to our spiritual lives. God knows the best place for us to be is completely and wholly in obedience to Him. In order to bring this about in us, He puts us in situations and places where we will be forced to choose between His power and ours. In those moments, it may be painful and may even produce tears, but if we become real about the process and understand what God wants to do through it we will start to welcome the journey. We will start to recognize the deeper He cuts, the more passionate and fulfilled we become. When we can live in this place, we have taken the most important step in confronting apathy in our lives.

CONCLUSION

In order to "reboot" our lives and become a passionate follower of Jesus Christ, we must first confront the source of apathy in our lives. The source of apathy is depending on our own power as the source of our potential. Until we are willing to deal with this, none of the rest of what this book says will make sense. If we are willing to become real about ourselves, become real about God's power, and become real about the process, God can start to work on the "hardware" of our heart so we are ready to take some of the next steps we will discuss.

REFLECTION QUESTIONS

1. Apathy is an "absence or suppression of passion, emotion, or excitement." Do you think this is evident in the world around us?

2. Do you have a "technology graveyard" in your home or business? In this chapter, we talked about how our lives are similar to these pieces of technology because our "hardware" is broken. Do you believe this is true?

3. How often do you think about what powers the things around you? Why is it easier to think about what powers other things while we neglect questioning what powers our everyday actions and thoughts?

4. In this chapter, we talked about three reasons we may try to power our own life: intentional rebellion, success, and failure. How have you seen these three things played out in your own life?

5. The source of apathy was defined as depending on our own power as the source of our potential. Do you agree with this definition? If so, how have you seen it tangibly in your own life or the world around you?

6. Peter says that God's "divine power has given us everything we need for life and godliness." Do you really believe God is powerful and wants to demonstrate that power in your everyday life?

7. It is dangerous to treat God like an idea instead of a person. Have you seen this in your own life?

8. Which of the application steps below might be most difficult for you to practice? Why?

APPLICATION

1. BECOME REAL ABOUT OURSELVES – Honestly evaluate what powers your daily life. As you find places in which you are depending on your own power as the source of your potential, confess your need for God in those areas.

2. BECOME REAL ABOUT GOD – Write down a list of the things that worry you on a daily basis. Now think about how those worries might change if you recognized that God is present with you every moment of every day. Confess God's greatness over each one of those issues.

3. BECOME REAL ABOUT THE PROCESS – The rebooting of the hardware of our spiritual life is a long-term process. Take some steps to put reminders in your life of the need to depend on God every day.

Chapter 2

Fundamental Promises
REBOOTING THE PROMISES OF OUR SPIRITUAL LIFE

Recently, I was at a waterpark with my family. It was an indoor water park with a wave pool, hot tubs, splash pads, and of course water slides. My son, Judah, who is almost four years old, was enjoying the slides in the children's section of the park. This was his first time at a waterpark and he was cautiously figuring it all out. His cousins, who are his age, had been to this park before and had graduated from the slides in the children's section to riding some of the bigger slides, with fun twists and turns. In fact, one of my nieces went down the bigger slide a dozen times in a row.

So, after Judah had gotten comfortable enough on the little slides, I told him we were going to go try the big slide now. You could see he was a little uncomfortable with the idea, but we climbed the stairs to the top of the slide and stood in line. He watched his cousin go down the slide first. I stationed our family at the bottom of the slide so he would know someone was there to grab him when he got off. I explained how fun it would be and how to go down the slide the correct way.

Finally, the bored slide attendant announced in a monotone, halfhearted way that it was our turn. We walked up to the slide and I sat Judah down in the water. I reassured him how fun it would be and I got ready to give him a push when he started to cry and kick and arch his back. I tried to reassure him again, but it was no use. He was doing everything in his power to make sure he did not have to go down that slide. The slide attendant broke his stoic gaze and looked at us. Other people were behind us. I realized we would have to regroup before we tried again.

I pulled Judah off the slide and walked some distance away. I asked him what the problem was. He expressed through tears he did not want to ride the slide. When I asked him why, he said he did not like it, but I could tell it was just because he was afraid. I tried to express again how fun it was going to be and reassured him he would not get hurt in any way. So, we walked over to the slide again, with the exact same result.

At this point I was a little frustrated, but it was not just because he refused to go down the slide. What I was frustrated about is that he did not trust me. I started to ask him questions like: "Would daddy have you do anything that would bring you harm" and "do you understand daddy just wants you to do this because you will have so much fun" and "you know you can trust me, right?" But it was no use. Even though he would answer positively that he knew I would never put him in a place to get hurt, he still would not trust me to go down that slide. We tried one more time, but before we even got to the slide I knew it was a doomed endeavor.

We walked down the stairs and he went off to play elsewhere, but I just stood there still frustrated about the situation. Now, before you say to "cut the poor kid some slack," I was not really even frustrated *at* him, but *for* him. You see, the same reaction of fear and unwillingness to trust I saw in him in that moment is the same fear I grew up with constantly. I was a shy and fearful kid when I was young, and this caused me to miss out on a lot of fun things simply because I chose to give in to my fear. I had come full circle to understand what my dad probably felt when I was little, and it was frustrating because I loved my son and wanted the best for him. More importantly, in that moment, I sensed God saying that this is how He often feels with us.

In the last chapter, we talked about becoming real about God's power by confronting the source of apathy in our hearts. The source of apathy is depending on our own strength instead of God's. Unfortunately, even if you come to a place of understanding that "His divine power has given us everything we need for a godly life," we can still have a hard time applying this in our daily lives. Go back to the computer analogy with me. Imagine the "hardware" of our spiritual lives is where we choose to get our power from and the "programs" we run are the actions we take on a regular basis. Even if your "hardware" is running correctly and you have confessed your need for God's power, it can still be difficult to see this come out in passionate actions or "programs" in your life. It is just like Judah on the slide. He was willing to acknowledge I would not put him in danger while at the same time not trusting me to actually go down the slide. His beliefs did not transfer into action.

For most of us, this is the same place we reside in our spiritual lives, and it is producing hidden apathy and hypocrisy on a daily basis. You might have read the first chapter and been somewhat frustrated because you feel like you confess your need for God and God's greatness on a regular basis, but are still not living a passionate life for Jesus. The reason for this is we have missed out on dealing with the "operating system" of our spiritual lives.

If you are confused what an operating system is, basically it is the main program that, "after being initially loaded into the computer by a boot program, manages all the other programs in a computer."[19] There are many kinds of operating systems, but the two primary systems people use are Windows or Mac OS. Operating systems are the connection point between the hardware and software or programs of a computer. They manage things such as how a computer processes information, how computer memory is distributed, and how all the files are stored.[20]

I would argue that each one of us has an operating system of sorts from which our thoughts, feelings, and actions flow. Proverbs 4:23 acknowledges this "operating system" is our heart and warns us to "above all else, guard your heart, for everything you do flows from it." When we think, feel, speak, or act, we are not just acting on a whim; we are acting out of the "operating system" of our heart. For instance, in Luke 6:45 it says, "A good man brings good things out of the good stored up in his heart, and an evil man brings evil things out of the evil stored up in his heart. For the mouth speaks what the heart is full of."

The Bible says that the operating system of our life or our heart is corrupted and difficult to understand. In the garden of Eden, Adam and Eve turned their backs on God and decided to live in their own power and intentional rebellion against God, like we talked about in the first chapter. Because of their rebellion, sin entered into the human race. Sin has corrupted our hearts and made the heart "deceitful above all things, and desperately sick; who can understand it."[21]

An understanding of the corruption of the heart is necessary to our understanding of salvation. It is only when we are broken to have a new heart that we can surrender to God's grace through Jesus' death and resurrection and start a relationship with God.[22] But even after we start a relationship with God, our hearts can still present a problem. The greatest thing sin in our heart disrupts is our ability to discern our motivations or the "fundamental promises" we rely on.

Before we come to know Jesus Christ personally, our motivation is only for our own self-interests. Even the good things we do are ultimately to make ourselves look good or feel good. The Bible would say our lives are rooted in the operating system of the "flesh" from the time we are born and our acts flow out of this place. Galatians 5:19-21 lists some of the acts that come from our operating system being the flesh: "Sexual immorality, impurity and debauchery; idolatry and witchcraft; hatred, discord, jealousy, fits of rage, selfish ambition, dissensions, factions and envy; drunkenness, orgies, and the like." Before coming to faith in Christ, it would not be unusual for the acts of our life to look like this list because the main motivation of the "flesh" is to please ourselves.

Thankfully, after we come into a relationship with Jesus, we are no longer under the control of this sinful operating system. We are given a new operating system by God. It says in Romans 6:14, "Sin shall no longer be your master, because you are not under law, but under grace." In Romans 8:9 it says, "You, however, are not in the realm of flesh but are in the realm of the Spirit, if indeed the Spirit of God lives in you." The Holy Spirit gives us the ability to function out of a new operating system in our lives. We are brought from death to life and given the ability to have completely different motivations, thoughts, feelings, and actions.

Reading this might cause you to feel guilty. You might say, "Well, I think I am a Christian, but it still feels like my normal operating system is the flesh instead of the Spirit." Or it might not go that far, but you would like your operating system to be the Spirit all the time and you still see the flesh popping up in different ways in your everyday life. You might feel like the Apostle Paul in Romans 7:14-24 when he says:

We know that the law is spiritual; but I am unspiritual, sold as a slave to sin. I do not understand what I do. For what I want to do I do not do, but what I hate I do. And if I do what I do not want to do, I agree that the law is good. As it is, it is no longer I myself who do it, but it is sin living in me. For I know that good itself does not dwell in me, that is, in my sinful nature. For I have the desire to do what is good, but I cannot carry it out. For I do not do the good I want to do, but the evil I do not want to do—this I keep on doing. Now if I do what I do not want to do, it is no longer I who do it, but it is sin living in me that does it. So I find this law at work: Although I want to do good, evil is right there with me. For in my inner being I delight in God's law; but I see another law at work in me, waging war against the law of my mind and making me a prisoner of the law of sin at work within me. What a wretched man I am! Who will rescue me from this body that is subject to death?

Paul recognizes that before he came into a relationship with Jesus Christ, there was not a tension in him. He simply lived out of the operating system of the flesh, doing whatever he wanted to do. But when he came to know Jesus, a battle seemed to develop. He wanted to do what was right, but it always seemed like something else was at work in him. The battle between the flesh and Spirit caused him to do things he did not really want to do. He had let go of the flesh as his only operating system, but it did not seem like he could live in the operating system of the Spirit all the time.

I believe the majority of people, at least in Christian churches across America, would feel this tension on a somewhat regular basis and this is another main reason why apathy is so prominent in peoples' faith. Most Christians walk around in a constant sense of hypocrisy. On one hand, they truly do want to follow after God. They want to have a passionate relationship with God, but what they know about their heart in those private moments when they are alone makes it hard for them to believe they really are that passionate. They know the temptations toward laziness, lust, greed, power, and control that still wage war against their soul. Even though the Spirit does work through their lives sometimes, it seems like they often revert back to the flesh being their operating system. How could they ever claim to be passionate about God? More than that, how can they even be sure they are at peace with God on a daily basis?

This is the question Peter answers in the next section of 2 Peter 1. He explains that God's divine power is available to us because of "fundamental promises" that God offers us.

THE QUESTION OF PROMISE

Promises are powerful. Homrighausen defines promise as "an assurance given by someone to another." He says, "He who promises has the power to fulfill, and he who is to receive waits with anticipation. In a real sense, men live by promises!"[23] (Interpreter's Bible, p. 173) Whether we realize it or not, this is true. Our lives are run by the promises we believe. Every single day you think, feel, and do thousands of things. Most of the time we think these things are somewhat disconnected from one another. For instance, you might think that you getting mad at your friend late in the day is completely disconnected from a financial worry you were discussing with your parents earlier. Or the worry and anxiety you have at work during the day is disconnected from the struggle you and your spouse are having communicating with one another. Or the reason you are angry at your pastor about his message Sunday is disconnected from your adult child that has seemingly walked away from his faith. It is true that at face value they seem disconnected, but deep down most of the issues going on in our lives can be boiled down to a couple key issues. These issues almost always have to do with a struggle of which promises to believe.

In 2 Peter 1:4, Peter continues to speak to the church about how to have access to God's divine power. He says, "Through these he has given us his very great and precious promises." What does he mean by "through these?" If you look back at the previous verse, it ends by acknowledging that we can receive God's power because he "called us by his own glory and goodness." He did not have to give us the chance to be in relationship with Him. He did not have to give us access to His power. Yet, because of His own glory and goodness, He not only offered us relationship and power, but also His "great and precious promises."

What kind of promises? God established promises throughout the entire Bible. These came in the form of covenants. Covenants are an "oath-bound promise whereby one party solemnly pledges to bless or serve another party in some specified way."[24] Covenants started all the way back in the beginning with Adam. In Genesis 2:15-17, God promised Adam and Eve a perfect and content life in the Garden, if they simply would not eat of the tree of the knowledge of good and evil. After Adam and Eve broke this covenant, God gave the first prophecy in the Bible that is also a promise. He explains in Genesis 3:15 that the "seed of the woman," who we come to understand as Jesus in the New Testament, will ultimately destroy Satan's plans and redeem us from sin and death.

God's covenants continue throughout the rest of the Bible with many different people. God promises Noah that He will never destroy the earth again with a flood. God promises Abraham that He will make his descendants as numerous as the stars in the sky. During the wandering time in the wilderness, God made a covenant with Moses and gave the people the Ten Commandments and the Law. God made a covenant with David that His kingdom would never end. Ultimately, Jesus confirms that He is the fulfillment of the New Covenant. Through Jesus' death and resurrection, we could be brought back into relationship with God through His grace. In some of these covenants, there were stipulations. In other covenants, God unilaterally decided to bless his people.

Beyond God's covenants, the entire Bible contains a treasure trove of promises that God has given us. In 2 Timothy 3:16 Paul says, "All Scripture is God-breathed and is useful for teaching, rebuking, correcting, and training in righteousness, so that the servant of God may be thoroughly equipped for every good work." God has breathed out His scriptures in order to explain His great and precious promises to us.

Why did God give us these great and precious promises? According to Peter in 2 Peter 1:4, God gave us these promises "so that through them you may participate in the divine nature, having escaped the corruption in the world caused by evil desires." The phrasing of this verse has been confusing for some theologians throughout history. It sounds like Peter is promoting a way we can become God or some form of escapism, but the confusion is simply because Peter is using the language of the false teachers of the day to prove his point. An important word to the philosophers of the day was the word "corruption" or *phthora* in Greek. Michael Green says of this word, "The transitoriness of life, the pointlessness of it all, oppressed many of the best thinkers in antiquity (as it does today)."[25] This word represented the deep hole and apathy that comes with living life in this world. Peter is saying that through God's great and precious promises we can escape the pointless nature of life that comes through this battle waged in us between the flesh and the spirit.

What does this all mean for us? Remember how I said earlier that we all live based on promises? Everything you think, feel, and do is based on a promise you are believing. For instance, if you believe hard work pays off then you will work hard even when things get tough. If you believe you are not good enough, then you may be conscientious of how you dress or quiet when you should speak up. If you believe certain people are not as valuable as others you will treat them differently. Think through a normal day and the motivations behind what you do. Why did you do everything you did today? In that "why" you will discover the promises you are believing.

Peter explains the power of God's promises in 2 Peter 1. He says that if we live according to God's great and precious promises, we can leave behind a hypocritical and apathetic life. But unfortunately, there is a struggle within us between God's great promises and our promises. It is almost like we are trying to work in God's "operating system" after we have been accustomed to working in our own "operating system" for a long time.

My earliest memory of a home computer was an old Apple computer connected to a box-like display. It was massive and plain. As a young child, it would have been a pretty amazing undertaking for me to even lift the display because of how heavy it was. I remember turning it on and hearing an electronic hum that continued as the background noise while you worked on the computer. In comparison to today's computers, it is funny to look back at how different things were back then from a hardware perspective.

The one thing that has not changed in the years since I used that first computer is the kind of operating system I use. The computer was an Apple computer, so it had a Mac operating system. There are many differences between operating systems. Some of the differences are behind the scenes; things that the majority of people would not really understand or recognize. The main tangible difference almost everyone can recognize is called the GUI or "Graphical User Interface." It is the way you interact with the computer and it is different depending on the operating system. For instance, an Apple computer organizes information differently, uses different commands, and has a different look than a Windows computer.

For whatever reason, my family has always been an Apple computer family. In present times, Apple has become the world's most valuable company and a huge player in not only computers, but phones, tablets, and other technology. Back in the day, though, Apple was dwarfed by Microsoft and its Windows operating system. I lovingly call my early years when I first remember using technology the "Apple dark ages." So, whenever I went to some place outside my home, I would almost always have to use a Windows computer because that is what most people had. You never truly realize how different operating systems are until you try to use a different kind.

Whenever I logged into a Windows computer at another person's house or at school, I was always so confused. Although many things looked similar, the commands were different, the way to access information and files was different, and the overall structure was different. Even after I got accustomed to using Windows computers when I needed to, I would still have a tendency to type the Mac OS commands that I was used to using.

This is similar to the question of promise in our lives. According to Ephesians 2:1-3, before we came to know Jesus Christ we were "dead in our transgressions and sins." We followed the promises of this dead life; simply giving into the "cravings of our flesh" and following "its desires and thoughts." We followed the promises of pleasure, wealth, power, and selfishness and found nothing at the end of that journey except pain and death. Yet, our operating system or heart was stuck in this position. It was all we knew.

But, "because of his great love for us, God, who is rich in mercy, made us alive with Christ even when we were dead in transgressions" and allowed us access to a new operating system.[26] You see, before we come to know Jesus our "flesh" is alive, but our spirit is dead. After coming to know Jesus, God brings our spirit to life and puts the "flesh" to death. You might say, "But that doesn't make any sense, because I have started a relationship with Jesus and I am trying to live passionately for Him, but it seems like my 'flesh' is alive and well. I am always fighting a battle to live for God and not fall away to temptation."

What if the operating system of the flesh is not alive and active, but we keep treating it like it is? What if God has disabled the operating system of the flesh in us and installed His Spirit in us, but we just don't know how to access it correctly? Similar to me trying to use a Windows computer after being used to Mac OS, we keep trying to use the same "commands" and follow the same "rules" and it does not work. We must learn and trust the new operating system.

There are two theological terms important to understand here. The first is justification. Justification is what happens when you surrender to God's grace by repenting from your sins and believing what Jesus did through His death on the Cross and the resurrection. You are declared righteous before God even when you did not deserve it. You are changed in that moment to become a new creation. You are no longer defined by your sin and flesh. Your flesh is now dead and your Spirit is alive. Romans 5:1 says, "Therefore, since we have been justified through faith, we have peace with God through our Lord Jesus Christ." If we were to look at our faith from this perspective, then it would make sense that when we come to know Christ, we would be perfect and there would no longer be any reason to sin.

This is where the other theological term comes in: sanctification. Jenney says, "In Christian theology, sanctification is usually understood as an act or process subsequent to salvation which renders the believer holy in fact."[27] Sanctification is the process that takes place to make the promise of justification a reality. So, justification is the great fundamental promise we are given; we are made right with God and He will never hold our sin against us again. We have been given a new operating system, a new set of rules, and a new way of living. But, sanctification is the process of learning to use this new operating system and unlearn the old operating system.

Why should this bring us hope? Well, for most of us we have believed our own version of faith instead of God's. We say things like, "God has been gracious to me, but I am still screwed up and just trying to live every day the best I can." Or we say things like, "No matter how hard I try, I will never escape this temptation in my life." Or we may even say things like, "I know people say this whole Jesus thing should change me, but I do not feel much different than I did before. Maybe it's not even real." If we depend on these false promises, then no wonder we have apathy in our spiritual lives. There is no hope in them. We are doomed to suffer through life, fighting a continuously losing battle because we are believing a half-truth.

If instead, we depend on the "very great and precious promises" of God, then there is great hope. Why did I call the former statements half-truths? Well, it is true we do not instantly become perfect in every action we take from the moment we become a Christian. And I am not saying you will never have to deal with temptation. What I am saying is that when we fall into temptation and sin after coming to know Jesus, it is not because this is who we are, it is because we have forgotten the fundamental promise of God: that we have been given a new operating system as a "child of God."

I came to know Jesus at a young age. I tried and tried to follow God in every way I could think of. In fact, by middle school I had read through most of the Bible, was involved in volunteer ministry, and tried to live a holy life as best I could. Yet, I was not at peace and had no joy. I was constantly guilty, thinking I had not done enough and worried if I did screw up God would punish me somehow. And ironically, despite me trying to live a holy life, the more I tried, the more often I would fall into temptation. It was a terrible way to live and I was confused. Despite doing everything I thought I was supposed to do, I did not feel like a passionate follower of Jesus Christ.

Finally, in the midst of junior high, I started to recognize my problem. Even though I had honestly come to know Jesus earlier in my life, I did not really understand what my decision meant. Despite God showing me grace, I was still living out of my own "promises" for my life instead of God's promises. Primarily, I did not trust that God had truly forgiven my sins once and for all. I did not believe I was truly accepted by God and that He would never leave me nor forsake me.[28] And I did not believe my true identity was now a "child of God," who desired to follow after God and live for Him. I constantly lived under a cloud of condemnation, waiting for the hammer to drop.

But, by the grace of God, I started to truly understand His promises to me. Here are some of God's great and precious promises to us:

- Romans 8:1 – "Therefore, there is now no condemnation for those who are in Christ Jesus."
- Romans 6:11 – "In the same way, count yourselves dead to sin but alive to God in Christ Jesus."
- 1 John 3:1 – "See what great love the Father has lavished on us, that we should be called Children of God."
- John 1:12 – "Yet to all who did receive Him, to those who believe in his name, he gave the right to become children of God."
- Romans 8:16 – "The Spirit himself testifies with our spirit that we are God's children."
- 2 Corinthians 3:17 – "Now the Lord is the Spirit, and

where the Spirit of the Lord is, there is freedom."

- Galatians 5:1 – "It is for freedom that Christ has set us free. Stand firm, then, and do not let yourselves be burdened again by a yoke of slavery."
- Romans 8:28 – "And we know that in all things God works for the good of those who love him, who have been called according to his purpose."

This is God's operating system for us. He wants freedom and love and joy for us. Far too often, however, we sit in apathy in our spiritual lives because we have chosen to listen to our own "promises" instead of depending on God's promises.

This struggle is like me standing there with Judah in front of the water slide. I so badly wanted him to understand the promises that I as his father could give him. I wanted him to understand that I was for him and not against him. I wanted him to know I desired good things for him, not bad. Just like Judah, we must make a choice of whether we will depend on our own "promises" or depend on God's promises for our life.

HOW TO DO THIS?

So how do we live in God's operating system instead of our own on a daily basis? The short answer is we must become rooted in the truth. If we do not come to terms with believing right things about God and ourselves, we will never be able to live out the life He desires for us.

So how do we become rooted in the truth? Well, interestingly enough, an operating system has a set of commands called "root" commands. According to the Linux Information Project, "root is the user name or account that by default has access to all commands and files on a Linux or other Unix-like operating system. It is also referred to as the root account, root user and the superuser."[29] Basically, if you are the root user you have complete control over the operating system. You can change anything you would like.

From a spiritual perspective, we could call these root commands the fundamental promises of our life. These are the things that we base all of our thoughts, feelings, and actions on. From the beginning of our life, we are the root user or superuser. We are in charge of the fundamental promises that shape our everyday actions. But after we come to know Jesus, we must let God become the root user again. We must let Him dictate the fundamental promises of our life.

We do this by a process detailed in Ephesians 4:22-24. It says, "You were taught, with regard to your former way of life, to put off your old self, which is being corrupted by its deceitful desires; to be made new in the attitude of your minds; and to put on the new self, created to be like God in true righteousness and holiness." So, we must take off the old, be made new in the attitude of our minds, and put on the new.

First, we must take off the old. Initially, in our lives this is the act of repentance. Part of starting a relationship with Jesus means we turn away from our sinful way of living. I often talk to people struggling with temptation and they say they want to live differently. I even hear them pray and ask God to change them. But when I ask them what they have done to turn away from the sin they struggle with, they say nothing. For instance, they have a pornography addiction, but they have done nothing to change the patterns, habits, and actions of their life. Or they have money problems, but they do nothing to eliminate their access to credit cards and other means of spending money. Now, if they ultimately have no desire to turn away from their sinful life, then I question whether they have ever truly started a relationship with Jesus.

If they sincerely do want to change but have not done anything to take off the old self, then I explain how this is a necessary step to becoming rooted in the truth. If we truly want to live by God's promises instead of our own, we must be willing to turn our back on the flesh. Remember how I said earlier that when we come to know Christ, the flesh is dead but the spirit is alive? This is the irony of us not wanting to take the old self off. It is already dead. I often tell people it is like we keep saying we cannot get away from our old self or temptation, when all it really is, is a dead body on our back. It has no power over us. It is simply like the rotting flesh of our former life hanging onto us. We must take off the old, dead self.

To do this we must first observe what is causing brokenness in our lives and take radical measures to remove that temptation from our life. For instance, installing accountability software on a computer, cutting up the credit cards, eliminating access to abused substances, avoiding media or entertainment that is not good for us, leaving an unhealthy friendship for a time, etc. If we were to just cut ourselves off from these things in our life and not do the following two steps there would be no lasting change in our lives. But we must first take off the old self in order to leave room for God to work.

Second, we must be made new in the attitude of our minds. This is something God must do for us. It is like God updating our operating system with his commands. Romans 12:2 says, "Do not conform to the pattern of this world, but be transformed by the renewing of your mind. Then you will be able to test and approve what God's will is – his good, pleasing, and perfect will." If we are to understand what God's truth is for our lives and become rooted in it, we must keep asking Him to transform our minds to be able to understand what His will is for us. When we were children we believed many things about the world, but as we got older we started to realize things are actually different than we originally believed. In the same way, we must be willing to give God access to everything we believe and invite Him to transform those beliefs into His beliefs.

How do we do this? Well, back to the example of the operating system and the root user, The Linux Information Project says, "The use of the term root for the all-powerful administrative user may have arisen from the fact that root is the only account having write permissions (i.e., permission to modify files) in the root directory."[30] Basically, the root user, or administrator of the operating system is the only one that can modify the files located on the computer. In the same way, if we are asking God to be the all-powerful administrative user of our life, we must make sure He is the only one modifying files.

On any given day, you have a thousand different voices coming at you trying to modify the things you think, feel, and believe. From the moment you wake up and check your phone through evening where you sit watching a movie, you are being bombarded by advertisements, entertainment, opposing worldviews, and many other things that can shape what you think and believe.

If you are wanting to be made new in the attitude of your mind, then you must intentionally and consistently set aside time to let God speak over the noise. This could look many different ways. You can start taking time to read the Bible and pray every morning before you do anything else. You could attend worship services every single week instead of missing consistently. You could spend time in the car turning off the radio and instead talking to God. You could meet up with a friend and accountability partner on a regular basis to talk about your spiritual walk. You could watch sermons while you are working on a project at home or cooking dinner. You could set aside times of solitude and silence to listen to God. You could fast from something for a time in order to leave room for God to speak. You could receive Christian counseling. Basically, you must leave room for God to renew and transform your mind by consistently and intentionally setting aside times to meet with Him.

Finally, as we take off the old and become renewed in the attitude of our minds, we must also put on the new self. As we take off the old self with its thoughts and actions, then leave room for God to change us, and start doing new actions that reflect the change God has brought about in us. Maybe instead of complaining, we start to intentionally give God thanks. Or, even if money seems to be tight for you, you intentionally start to tithe and trust God to provide what you need. This will be addressed more thoroughly in the next chapter, but it is important to recognize that part of depending on God's fundamental promises is having our actions ultimately change.

CONCLUSION

In the first chapter, we discussed how apathy begins when we decide to depend on our own power instead of God's power. I hope you have recognized that even if we let God reboot our idea of power, we must also let Him reboot the operating system of our heart, or the fundamental promises we believe. This comes about when we recognize our true identity in Jesus and become rooted in the truth by choosing to take off the old self, become renewed in the attitude of our minds, and put on the new self. In the next chapter, we will look into more of what it means to let God reboot the practices of our life.

REFLECTION QUESTIONS

1. Have you ever been in a situation like the story at the beginning of this chapter? Have you ever wanted to do something but did not trust the person you were with enough to take the risk?
2. An operating system is the connection point between the hardware and programs of a computer. We talked about how our hearts are the operating system of our life. Did this make sense or not? If not, why not? Proverbs 4:23 and Luke 6:45 are good reference points if needed.
3. Sin in our heart disrupts our ability to discern our motivations or the "fundamental promises" we rely on. Do you see evidence of this in your life or the lives of others around you?
4. Our lives are controlled by the operating system of the flesh before we come to know Jesus. After we come to know Jesus, we are then controlled by the operating system of the Spirit. Unfortunately, there is still a tension in us between the flesh and spirit that the Apostle Paul describes in Romans 7. Have you seen this tension in your own life?
5. 2 Peter 1:4 says, "Through these, he has given us his very great and precious promises so that through them you may participate in the divine nature, having escaped the corruption in the world caused by evil desires." What are some of God's promises for us?
6. Think through your day. Why did you do everything you

did today? Did you depend on God's promises for your day or your own?

7. Which of the application steps below might be most difficult for you to practice? Why?

APPLICATION

1. PUT OFF THE OLD SELF – Repent of sinful patterns and actions in your life by deliberately turning away from them. This may mean putting accountability software on your computer, cutting up a credit card, etc.

2. BE MADE NEW IN THE ATTITUDE OF YOUR MIND – Intentionally put yourself in a place to let God shape your heart. Examples would include daily prayer and Bible reading, worship services, tithing, etc.

3. PUT ON THE NEW SELF – As you start to depend on God's promises, actively take steps of faith to practice what He has promised.

Chapter 3

Effectively Ineffective
REBOOTING THE PRACTICES OF OUR
SPIRITUAL LIFE

I have always had a love/hate relationship with technology. When I watch the commercials for a piece of technology or listen to their advertisements, technology has always had an appeal to me. The essential message of most computer or technology commercials is that this technology will make your life more effective, productive, fun, successful, enjoyable, etc. Many times this is a tempting message to me. I think, "How great would it be to have my life be more successful or productive or enjoyable?"

The problem is that, most often, technology has made my life more complicated and less productive. I think back to when I was given a palm pilot. Some younger readers might not even know what those are anymore. I was in high school at the time and I thought my palm pilot would make life more effective and productive. I mean I could keep track of notes and use it for my calendar and many other things. Instead, the most memorable use I had for it was to use it to turn TV's on and off. I was fascinated with this one application that allowed the palm pilot to become a universal remote. In fact, in the middle of a band rehearsal one time I decided to turn on the TV over the band director's head. Obviously, this technology was not making my life more productive, but instead was getting me into trouble.

In junior high, I was really passionate about selling discount cards for a band fundraiser (yes, this is now two stories in a row about being in band, which probably qualifies me as a band nerd) because I really wanted to get the prize money. The reason I desperately wanted this money was to spend it on a new handheld video game device. I went door to door and tried my best to sell these discount cards even though I was a terrible salesman. Surprisingly, I ended up winning the prize money. I bought the video game device and was so excited that my life would now be more enjoyable. Unfortunately, within only a couple of weeks, I realized the game was fun but took me away from doing other fun things. I rarely played with it again.

In the past decade, in particular, I have watched this issue become increasingly more difficult for me. And honestly I think many, if not most, people today struggle with wasting time and energy on devices. I got an iPhone many years ago and there are definitely ways it has helped me to be more productive. But I find it so interesting how it has made my life both more and less productive at the same time. Sure, I can search for any little fact I need to know in an instant, yet how many times has that search turned from important research to ending up on a page about the life expectancy of a rare bird in the jungles of Central America. Or, I can watch important videos on YouTube about Bible teachers and theological issues and then the next second be watching a video about how to use Mentos to cause a soda bottle to erupt. Or, I can use my phone as a powerful communication tool where I can counsel people going through tough times or use it to isolate myself in the midst of a waiting room by checking football scores or scrolling Facebook.

Computers, TV's, phones, watches, tablets: we are surrounded by tools promising effectiveness and productivity and yet they more often than not cause us to become less effective. Here's the thing, though. I am not sure this distraction is unwanted. I am convinced that often we are more than happy to be effectively ineffective. As we discussed earlier in the book, there are usually three scenarios in which we allow apathy to swallow up our lives: success, failure, or intentional rebellion. So, whether we are rewarding ourselves for being successful or pitying ourselves for being a failure or intentionally desiring to waste our time and lives, we often look for ways to be effectively ineffective. And this is the problem at the heart of the next issue we are going to examine.

So far in the book we have looked at the source of apathy, which is depending on our own power for the source of our potential. Then, we looked at the fundamental promises we believe that shape our heart or the operating system of our lives. In this third chapter, we are going to look at the part of apathy that almost everyone recognizes when it goes wrong, but we rarely know how to deal with it: when apathy impacts the practices of our life or our everyday actions, thoughts, and feelings.

I am convinced most of us live effectively ineffective lives. On the one hand, we want to do amazing things for God and live out a life like Jesus, but on the other hand we intentionally sabotage our own effectiveness. Peter addresses this issue next in 2 Peter 1. In verse 8, after talking about several practices Christians should exhibit, he says, "For if you possess these qualities in increasing measure, they will keep you from being ineffective and unproductive in your knowledge of our Lord Jesus Christ." So, the increasing production of righteous thoughts, attitudes, and actions will keep us from ineffectiveness.

In the next verse, he acknowledges what happens when we choose to not practice these things: "But whoever does not have them is nearsighted and blind, forgetting that they have been cleansed from their past sins." When we refuse to actually practice what we have learned from our relationship with God, we are exposing the fact that we have a seeing problem. We have lost sight of the grace of God in our lives. We have become engrossed in the things of this world and turned our back on the things of God.

Peter's call to the Christians of the time in 2 Peter 1:10 is, "Therefore, my brothers and sisters, make every effort to confirm your calling and election." Peter says godly practices are an essential part of our Christian life. Sometimes, I think apathy in people's lives comes from this scary and incorrect belief that since God has provided His grace for their sins, they have license to do whatever they want. They rationalize their sinful actions away by believing God has promised to forgive them no matter what they do. The false teachers of Peter's day were living this kind of life. They were focused on their theological debates and beliefs, but did not actually live godly lives. Instead, Peter essentially says, "the acid test of the genuineness of our faith is that either we make costly life changes on the basis of it, or we treat sin and judgment as irrelevant to a Christian."[31]

You might say, "But that sounds like we need to earn our faith? I thought we could not do anything to earn salvation before God?" This is true and it brings up an essential distinction we must make when we are bringing up the practices of our life.

BEING AND DOING

One of the great confusions of living a passionate life for God comes down to a misunderstanding of God's responsibility and our responsibility in our spiritual growth. Many spend all their time striving to earn the grace of God. Others end up saying only God can help them do the right things so they sit and wait for Him to make them do what is right. Both of these extremes are wrong and lead to apathy for different reasons, one because of a misunderstanding of salvation and the other because of a misunderstanding of relationship.

So far in the book, we have focused on the importance of being or becoming. This is the essential beginning point of a relationship with Jesus. If we believe what the Bible says about God, sin, and salvation then it becomes clear that we are broken, in and of ourselves, unable to have a right relationship with God. We cannot *do* something good enough to please God. It is only when we surrender to God's grace by believing in Jesus's death and resurrection and confessing Him as the Lord of our life that God does the work to save us.

After this, growing in our relationship with Jesus only comes about by being with Him and becoming like Him. For instance, if we consider the computer analogy we have been using, as we surrender the "hardware of our life" or our power to Him, He starts to empower us to live a godly life. We simply need to become real about who we are, who God is, and the process He uses to help us grow. After this, in order for the "operating system of our lives," our heart, to work according to God's intentions, we must become rooted in His truth and identity for us instead of our own. All of this happens as a result of God working in us, not us achieving it on our own.

Yet, as you probably already recognized, even though God is the one to do the ultimate work in us, we have a job as well. Our job is not to *do* the work that needs to be done. Our job is to intentionally and consistently *allow* God's work to be done in and through us. As we open the door of our heart, God walks through. As we follow in His footsteps, He leads us to where He wants us to go. As we open up space for Him to work, He mends and heals and empowers.

Think of it like this: the practices of our life or the things we do, think, and feel are the applications or programs of our life. A computer may have good hardware and a good operating system, but if it does not have any applications or programs to run, what use is it anyway? A computer or other piece of technology was created for a purpose: to be effective and useful. In the same way, although it is essential we have the right hardware and a right operating system, we were ultimately created for a purpose and a reason. Ephesians 2:10 says, "For we are God's handiwork, created in Christ Jesus to do good works, which God prepared in advance for us to do." We were created to fulfill God's purposes and plans. We were created to have an impact on this world. We were created to be useful and effective in the hands of God, so all people may know His power and love.

So how do we fulfill this plan for our lives? Do we just passionately start doing as much good as we can and try to eliminate as much evil from our lives as possible? Well, if the practices of our lives are like programs on a computer, can a computer just start adding programs on their own? A computer might be able to, on its own, automatically update some programs here and there (although even this is simply because the programmer has written it into the code). But the only way a computer can truly get rid of old and outdated programs, update programs, and add new programs is to let itself be open to the actions of the user.

Remember how we talked about God being like the "root user" or "system administrator" of our lives in the last chapter? Think of it like this. For the "programs of our life" or practices of our life to truly change, God uses the "hardware of our life" to update the "programs of our life" through the "operating system of our life." Or, put another way, when we surrender to the power of God He starts to change the practices of our life by changing our heart.

Now, sometimes this happens without us even really understanding it. For instance, I have heard many stories of people walking into a church service with a serious addiction or sin issue in their life. That day the truth of God's Word made sense to them even though it had not on other occasions. In response to the call of God, they surrendered the control of their sin issue to God and let Him provide healing. Walking out of the church service, the actual practices of their life immediately changed. Instead of desiring nothing but that addiction or temptation, they now desired nothing more than to honor God. But, did the person *do* something to deal with their sin issue or did they *become* something? All they did was open their heart to the work of God and God did the work to change their practices.

So, we do have a role to play in shaping the practices of our life, but our role is not to change those practices in our power alone. Our job is to consistently and intentionally be open to God's work on the practices of our life and then to obediently walk it out.

WHY WE NEED A REBOOT

The problem comes for many of us after we have been in a relationship with God for a little while. You see, at the beginning of our relationship with God, we are so blown away by God's grace and love and are so excited to see how God is transforming us that we welcome God into almost any situation in our lives. We give Him the full reign to remove programs, update programs, and install new programs at His discretion. Although our practices are still a rough sketch of what we know God wants them to be, we can see that He is actively helping us to turn aside from temptation, to truly love people, and to leave behind things like worry and anxiety.

But the further we go in this process of spiritual growth, the deeper God goes into our "hard drives." For instance, when we first came to know God He "uninstalled" things that were destructive to our lives and hurt other people, so we were grateful. But the further we go in our spiritual walk, the more He starts to "uninstall" things we enjoy and want to hang on to. We rationalize them and make them out to be okay, even though God says the practice is not something He wants us to act on anymore.

Or maybe when God first started to work in our lives, we were excited about some of the new programs He was installing. People could tell a distinct difference in our lives as we started to love people around us more with our words and actions. But the further we go in our spiritual walk, God starts to install more intense programs. We know if we agree to practice these things that it will be uncomfortable and difficult. We rationalize this away by trying to tell God about all the programs He has already installed and how far we have come. We say to God, "Haven't we come far enough?"

And this is where the practices of our spiritual lives become apathetic or effectively ineffective. Moffatt poignantly expresses a cynic's response to this process in our spiritual lives when he describes it as "an initial spasm followed by chronic inertia."[32] We decide we are content in our life and we are not sure we want God to take us any further. We still practice good things for the most part. And even if there are some bad practices in our life, we become masters at rationalizing them away. We say things like, "Well, I am still struggling with that same old problem, but we are all human, aren't we?" Or we say something like, "I have been working so hard to honor God with everything else, it's okay to take care of me for a little bit." Or we give any one of a thousand rationalizations for why it is okay to stop letting God change our practices, but what we do not realize is there is no middle ground.

We imagine that if we stop letting God continue to do His work in our life, then we will be able to just keep using the programs we have in the same way going forward. We imagine we can keep growing and having a transformed life; it will just happen on our timetable instead of God's. The problem with this is, if we stop letting God have access to the "programs" of our life, then he will not be able to update them like they need to be. Without knowing it, we will start to devolve into an increasingly ineffective follower of Christ.

If you have ever owned a computer or phone or other piece of technology you know what I mean. I tend to be that guy who never really updates their phone or computer unless it becomes absolutely necessary. I am not sure whether it is just laziness or an overactive sense of flexibility, but I tend to keep hitting the "remind me later" button when it asks me if I want to update my operating system or a program. I keep hitting the button until one day when I go to start the program or app, it says it will not even run anymore unless I update it. Without fail, every time I do update the program I say, "Man, this is so nice how they've updated everything. I wonder why I waited so long to update it?" You see, companies update programs because they are always finding bugs to repair or figuring out ways to make the programs even more effective. When I choose to keep hitting "remind me later," I am not just staying at the same level of effectiveness with my technology. I am missing out on the good things that could make me more effective and if I keep stalling I may not be able to even use the program anymore.

We have people come to us on a regular basis at the church with a broken marriage, a serious sin issue, or some other brokenness in their life and they sometimes say, "How could this have happened? I thought I was doing the same things I have always done?" My heart breaks for them because they have failed to recognize they kept hitting "remind me later" to God's updates and they did not realize the practices of their life would become effectively ineffective when they continued to do this.

Whether you have come to the end of your rope like these people have or you are mostly allowing God access to the practices of your life, all of us could use a reboot of the practices of our life. Every moment of every day there are things that, if we simply let God have access to them, He will start to update them to be more effective for His glory and for our good. The question is, what kind of updates does God want to make in our lives?

WHAT PRACTICES?

In the midst of 2 Peter 1, Peter gives us a list of things that God wants added to our lives. This is not a necessarily unique list or a complete list. There are several other lists within the New Testament that guide us in ways God wants the practices of our life to look different than the world around us. But this list gives us a good idea of some of the main practices God wants in our lives.

In verses 5-7, he says, "For this very reason, make every effort to add to your faith goodness; and to goodness, knowledge; and to knowledge, self-control; and to self-control, perseverance; and to perseverance, godliness; and to godliness, mutual affection; and to mutual affection, love." He emphasizes we are to make every effort to have these practices in our lives and we are to add these to our faith. As we have already discussed, "making every effort" and "adding to our faith" are simply ways of expressing we are consistently and intentionally offering up the practices of our life to God, receiving the updates He wants to make, and obediently walking out those practices. As Lucas and Green say, "We are to cooperate with God, working with him without thinking of the price."[33]

Faith

The first practice described is faith. Faith is essential to the working out of all other practices. Only faith in what God has done and what God will continue to do will bring about movement in the other areas of our life. Think of faith as the

"Finder" program on a computer. On a Mac OS computer, the "Finder" program is the essential program that is always open and allows you to use the other applications. This program is the main screen where you can access the hard drive to see what documents and applications you have, where you can select the other programs you would like to run, and where you can access all the important information about the computer. People often think that "Finder" is a part of the operating system and it is, but it is also a program that is running. In a similar way, "Faith is to be both foundational and functional."[34]

Faith is the foundation of our relationship with Jesus and our identity in Him. But it is also active and functional. When God calls out a practice in our life He would like to remove, update, or add, faith must be enacted in order to allow God to do His work. A lot of times, the changes God wants to make to our lives do not make sense to us because we have never experienced them before. Faith is functional when we choose to trust Him over the fear or discomfort that comes with practices changing in our life.

Goodness

Peter next turns his attention to goodness. Goodness was an important term in that day among the philosophers and thinkers. It was reflective of the search for "what is the excellence of man?"[35] Basically, what is the ultimate example of a human being? Peter's response is different than the thinkers of his day. They had many other ideas, but his idea was that of "Christlikeness." If Jesus lived a perfect life as a man, then our ultimate goodness would be the imitation of Jesus. Thus, goodness could be summarized by evaluating whether the actions of our lives reflect the old statement from many years ago, "What would Jesus do?" When I am with my family, at work, having fun, writing an email, having a meal with a friend, am I doing what Jesus would do?

Think of goodness like an emulator program. An emulator program has been described as "when one system imitates or reproduces another."[36] These are programs written specifically for you to access programs not native to your operating system. For instance, on a Mac computer, there is an emulator that allows you to run programs as if your computer was a Windows computer. In the same way, when we ask ourselves "what would Jesus do" we are seeking to imitate or emulate the way of our God. As it says in 1 Peter 2:21, "To this you were called, because Christ suffered for you, leaving you an example that you should follow in his steps." We were called to walk in His steps, living like He lived every moment of every day.

This sounds easy, but we know it is not always as easy as it sounds. I think the most difficult part of following in Jesus' steps is that we get confused as to what He actually would do in certain situations. For instance, movies, the internet, fast food, cars, grocery stores, and so many other modern issues did not exist in Jesus' day. We are faced with challenges and circumstances daily that seem so out of context with what Jesus dealt with. And many people have countless opinions on what it means to be a good person. This is why goodness so clearly connects with the next practice: knowledge.

Knowledge

Knowledge is an essential element to our faith. If you want to follow God and become a passionate follower of Jesus

Christ, you must desire to know what the Bible says about who He is. Talking to people over the years, many say they are a passionate follower of Jesus, but at the same time say they are not much of a reader and have never gotten into the Bible. Immediately, red flags go off in my spirit, because there are few things more dangerous than a person who says they are a follower of Jesus who does not read the Bible.

I usually equate it to any other pursuit to show how silly it would be for us to call ourselves a passionate follower of Jesus when we do not desire to know the Bible. For instance, would you be comfortable having a surgeon perform a procedure on you who has said they are not a reader and did not read their textbooks? Would you trust that a boyfriend or girlfriend is really in love with you if they never took time to read your letters, emails, or texts? Would you trust someone who said they were passionate about a hobby if they never studied it? The clear answer is no. The reality is you study what you are passionate about, no matter what it is. It is essential we know what the Bible says, if we want to walk in Jesus' steps.

There are some of you reading this who have studied the Bible extensively. In fact, you have taken almost every class your church offers on the Bible. You may have even taught classes on the Bible, but still do not have a clear practice of knowledge in your life. This is because knowledge is not just about how much you study, but how that knowledge ties to life. It is good to know about the trumpets and bowls in the book of Revelation, but do you know how to reach out to the homeless living near you? It is good to know the theme of the book of Hosea, but do you know how to love your spouse well? It is good to know the names of the twelve disciples, but do you know how to lovingly encourage someone else to take steps in their faith?

You see, as Scottish preacher John Brown said, "This knowledge means 'making a distinction not only between what is true and what is false but also between what is right and wrong – what is becoming and unbecoming – what is advantageous and hurtful'"[37] With a rudimentary reading of the Bible and study of some other books, it is relatively easy to figure out what is true and what is false about the world around us. (If you are struggling with figuring this out and you have many doubts, I encourage you to start reading the Bible together with someone you trust and asking them questions about it. Also, I would encourage you to seek out books, videos, and other resources from great apologetic teachers like Ravi Zacharias and William Lane Craig.) The more difficult question for us is how to respond to the world.

For instance, it is not difficult to figure out what love is when you study 1 John 4, but it is far more difficult to know how to love people around you with God's love. Or it is not difficult to understand how broken the world is when we see what the Bible has to say about sin, but it is far more difficult to know how to respond to our broken world. This knowledge is not just intellectual knowledge, but applied knowledge.

So how do we go about "making every effort" to add practical knowledge to our life? Well, think of this practice like a web browser on your computer or phone. It is an amazing phenomenon in the history of mankind that we live in a time when you can have a random question about anything and you can find an answer in a split second by opening the web browser on your phone or computer. And the magnitude of the internet seems daunting, almost endless. Literally any question you can think of is at the push of a few keys, or with the advent of voice-activated assistants like Siri or Alexa, at a simple spoken command.

Do you know God's knowledge makes the accumulated knowledge of the internet look like child's play? Listen to what it says in Romans 11:33-36:

Oh, the depth of the riches of the wisdom and knowledge of God! How unsearchable his judgments, and his paths beyond tracing out! Who has known the mind of the Lord? Or who has been his counselor? Who has ever given to God, that God should repay them? For from him and through him and for him are all things. To him be the glory forever! Amen.

You can never get to the end of God's wisdom and knowledge. There is not a situation you experience where God does not have an answer. More than that, He says in James 1:5-8 that He wants to give you His wisdom:

If any of you lacks wisdom, you should ask God, who gives generously to all without finding fault, and it will be given to you. But when you ask, you must believe and not doubt, because the one who doubts is like a wave of the sea, blown and tossed by the wind. That person should not expect to receive anything from the Lord. Such a person is double-minded and unstable in all they do.

No matter what you face in your daily life, it is possible to have knowledge of God's will. The first step in learning what God desires is to read the Bible and study it. The second step which is just as important is to come to God every day in prayer and learn to listen to His voice. Whether it is a problem at home, at work, or at school, God will give us wisdom to deal with each situation if we ask Him in faith.

Self-Control

As we learn more about what God desires in our everyday life, it will lead us toward the practice of self-control. Self-control is a "mastery of the appetites." (Interpreter's Bible, p. 176) All of these practices are important, but if we were to choose one that most directly correlates with apathy in the modern Western world it would have to be self-control. Almost everything in our affluent society is sold to us as a fulfillment of an appetite. There are other parts of the world where they need self-control, but there is much less to have self-control about. For many people in the world, their concern is whether they will have food to eat for the day. Our concern is that we have become bored with the restaurant options we have on a given day of the week. For many people in the world, their concern is whether they will have enough money to pay for their children to attend school. Our frustration is that we do not have enough money in a certain pay period to buy that new outfit or new gadget we saw on an infomercial.

And in the Christian church, we have gone after certain areas of self-control, but have left others in the realm of personal preference. We have talked about the dangers of sexual appetites and for good reason. There is a unique danger in lack of control in our sexual appetites. 1 Corinthians 6:18-20 says:

Flee from sexual immorality. All other sins a person commits are outside the body, but whoever sins sexually, sins against their own body. Do you not know that your bodies are temples of the Holy Spirit, who is in you, whom you have received from God? You are not your own; you were bought at a price. Therefore honor God with your bodies.

There is a uniqueness in our sexual appetites because our bodies are involved. This means that lack of control in our sexual appetites has the ability to ruin our minds, our relationships, and even the way our body functions. Sex is a blessing of God designed for the context of marriage between a man and a woman. Any kind of fulfillment of a sexual appetite outside of that does serious damage to our life.

But as important as self-control in the midst of our sexual appetites is, there are many other areas of our life that necessitate the practice of self-control. A common topic for Jesus was the power of money and possessions to destroy us. He says in Luke 12:15, "Watch out! Be on your guard against all kinds of greed; life does not consist in an abundance of possessions." And although self-control in regard to money and possessions is discussed in the church, I think we discuss it the way we discuss eating cookies.

I do not think it is a surprise to most people that it is not a good idea to eat cookies all the time at every meal. That is why it is funny to me to hear people discuss dieting about things like cookies. I would not be surprised at all to see a group of people standing at a party and have one person say, "Yeah, I was just reading this article about how cookies are loaded with sugar." Another person might say, "I went off cookies for a couple days last week and I felt so much better." And still another person might say, "I so agree. We must be careful not to eat too many cookies." The irony of the whole situation is they are discussing all of this while standing at a birthday party eating cookies.

We might discuss the power of money and possessions in our lives, knowing these have the power to destroy us, but all the while not really taking any tangible steps to control the power of money and possessions in our lives. According to a

2016 report, the average credit card debt in American households is $16,883 and the average overall debt is $137,063.[38] Yet, we do not seem to connect the dots that this amount of debt can have serious consequences on our spiritual lives. Or maybe you do not have excessive debt, but you have countless possessions and still cannot get rid of the feeling that you need more. Now, I am not trying to produce a guilt trip for us. I am simply trying to explain the need for the practice of self-control in our lives for all things: sex, money, entertainment, hobbies, food, etc. When we do not have self-control, we miss out on the blessing of God.

So, how do we actually practice self-control? Think of it like the System Preferences on your computer. The System Preferences allow you to control where and when and how you interact with all the other elements on your computer. You set up the controls and from that point on your computer functions within those boundaries. This could include things like parental controls, access to certain types of files, how the computer is organized, and how often it goes to sleep.

The practice of self-control is very similar. In faith, based on the desire to imitate Jesus and the knowledge to understand how He wants us to do that, we set up our lives in such a way to act out that knowledge. Self-control does not just happen in the moment. Self-control takes vision in planning out your life.

For instance, any nutritionist would tell you that if you want to have self-control in your eating habits it takes planning. Imagine you start a day saying you really want to eat healthy, but you did not plan out anything to eat for any of your meals nor time to eat for that matter. Then you have a busy day at work or at home. What usually happens? You start your day, skip lunch because you are busy, then get to the evening and you are starving. But you say to yourself, "I am practicing self-control." So, you try really hard to resist the bag of unhealthy potato chips in the corner. You try to eat something healthy, only to later grab the bag of potato chips and eat half of them. Maybe this has not happened to you in the area of food, but the same principle can be played out in any area of life. The practice of self-control takes planning out your life in order to live effectively for God.

Just like you might unselect certain options in your System Preferences, it might mean intentionally removing temptation from your daily life. It could be following God's wisdom in locking yourself out of certain aspects of your computer because you want to honor God with your sexual appetites and you know pornography is a struggle. It could be making a budget or cutting up your credit cards. It could be signing out of a certain form of social media because it is taking too much attention away from other important things in life. It could be removing your TV from your living room for a while to give yourself a break from the constant noise. It can take so many forms.

Just like you might select certain options in your System Preferences you would like to add to your experience, the practice of self-control might mean intentionally adding things into your life. For instance, our spiritual lives are not just about defensively staying away from bad things. In fact, more often than not, if we just try to live defensively we will fail. Instead, the more powerful action we can take is to intentionally add good patterns and habits into our lives.

For instance, you could add intentional time for your family to gather for a meal every night (without technology) in order to talk about your day and how God showed up that day. Or perhaps you make it an intentional habit to always encourage one person at work, no matter the situation. Or maybe you make it an intentional habit that if you buy something, you always give something away.

The practice of self-control is a necessity against apathy. But we must also remember what we have learned so far. If you simply take from this that you can go out in your own power and "promises" and practice self-control in order to destroy apathy, you are sorely mistaken. We must take the practice of self-control in the context of everything we have talked about thus far. As you surrender to God's power, understand His identity for you, and intentionally ask Him to work in your life, He will give you the power to be self-controlled. We must simply follow His lead and be obedient in laying out our lives in such a way to be self-controlled.

Perseverance

The practice of perseverance is the practice of looking beyond your present circumstances. Every day we are going to face some sort of adversity. In fact, Jesus says to His disciples in John 16:33, "In this world you will have trouble." In fact, we may face even more adversity in our lives after starting a relationship with Jesus than we did before. It is a principle of life that stagnant things like to stay stagnant or people that are apathetic like to stay apathetic.

Not only that, but we have an enemy who stands against us, not wanting us to fulfill our potential in Jesus Christ. In 1 Peter 5:8 it says, "Be alert and of sober mind. Your enemy the devil prowls around like a roaring lion looking for someone to devour." We should not be surprised to meet with some resistance in our journey of becoming a passionate follower of Jesus Christ.

For many people, however, I think they believe that when they start a relationship with Christ everything will be smooth sailing from that day forward. They get surprised when they start to face resistance. But, as was said, resistance does not change in our lives after we come to know God. In fact, it may get worse.

The hope we have is that before we came to know Christ we had no weapon or defense against adversity. We were grasping for whatever would make us feel good in the moment because we could not stand against the realities of life. But after we come to know Jesus, we now have access to the greatest person and greatest power in the universe. That is why Jesus follows up his dire statement in John 16:33 with, "But take heart! I have overcome the world." We now can stand in the midst of whatever comes our way.

The practice of perseverance is all about keeping the big picture and the end in mind, so you can stand strong amid whatever comes your way. Think about it like your calendar app on your computer or phone. It is what keeps the perspective of time in your life.

I am not sure if you have ever done this, but when I was starting my master's program it was an immediate temptation to get overwhelmed by the enormity of it all. I knew God had called me to pursue it, but the idea of starting an online/onsite master's program lasting three to four years while still working full-time in ministry and starting a family was daunting. It took a lot out of me and a lot from me: constant late nights, lack of a social life, lack of time to exercise, lack of mental energy in other areas of my life, and many other things. But at the end of the day I was able to persevere.

How? Well, first and foremost, it was by the grace of God. I needed to be dependent on Him every step of the way. But the other reason I was able to persevere was because I was able to put this time into context. In essence, I was able to pull out my calendar program and look at the big picture. I could see that God had called me to this and it was only three years of my life (which would go by very quickly). After each section of classes I was one step closer and it would be a great benefit to me in the big picture of my life.

So, the practice of perseverance is the practice of looking at the big picture. This is why it says in Colossians 3:1-4:

Since, then, you have been raised with Christ, set your heart on things above, where Christ is, seated at the right hand of God. Set your minds on things above, not on earthly things. For you died, and your life is now hidden with Christ in God. When Christ, who is your life, appears, then you will also appear with him in glory.

When we are able to set our hearts and minds on things above instead of the struggles of this present day, we find strength to persevere instead of giving up.

Godliness

As we begin to look beyond our present circumstance in order to persevere, it makes it much easier to practice godliness. Peter uses the word for godliness earlier in verse 3, but now refers to it in terms of practicing godliness. Green describes godliness as "a very practical awareness of God in every aspect of life."[39]

Have you ever pondered how interesting it is that many of us talk about being followers of God, but do not often believe He is a part of everyday life? For instance, we might go to church on Sunday and read our Bibles every morning, and yet not really recognize or think about God's presence during a stressful business proposal at work. Or we might set aside times to pray, but we do not think about God's presence during an argument with our teenager. No wonder we often have such narrow perspective and such little power in everyday temptation and conflict.

Imagine if we actually recognized God's presence daily. Imagine if we knew in faith He was listening in on every conversation, comforting us in the midst of every disappointment, pointing the direction when we feel lost, and cheering us on as we obediently love our enemies. The practice of godliness, or recognizing the presence of God and acting accordingly, is a powerful antidote to apathy.

How do we practice godliness? Well, think of it like the notifications on your phone or computer. For those who own a phone or computer, you know how constant notifications have become in our lives. They are the little notes that pop up on the side of our computer screen as we are working on something else. Or they are the reminders that pop up on our phone throughout the day. Sometimes, we may be frustrated by how many reminders come through on a regular basis distracting us from our day, but the irony is we are the ones who set them up.

What if we intentionally set up reminders of God's presence in our life? Some of these are simple, like attending church services and a small group every week without fail. I get concerned for someone who decides that weekly attendance at church is not a high priority in their life. They might say, "If I get there I get there, but I am still a passionate follower of Jesus." I might respond with the question, "You may be, but if you are so apathetic about being with the people of God, how long will you be a passionate follower of Jesus?"

See, there are many reasons why we attend church, but one of them is to have a constant reminder in community of God's presence in our lives. When people stop attending church weekly, the reality of God's presence in their everyday life can easily start to fade.

Intentional reminders of God's presence can take many other forms as well. For instance, posting certain Bible verses around your house or putting a note on your rearview mirror or setting a reminder on your phone or making it a habit to pray with your spouse before bed are great starts. The more we practice the presence of God, the more we will be able to practice the last two actions Peter talks about.

Brotherly Kindness and Love

The last two practices Peter refers to are two different words for love in Greek. The first is "philadelphia" which might sound familiar because the city in Pennsylvania of the same name is called "the city of brotherly love." The other word, "Agape," is the highest word used for love in the Bible. It is representative of God's love and "it is marked by its indiscriminate and deliberate habit of loving not just brothers but those outside the family circle too."[40]

Real love has the power to change anything. It was God's love that led Him to sacrifice Himself on our behalf so that we could have life. It has been love throughout the centuries that has stopped wars, freed captives, elevated slums, produced generosity, and changed the world system. Yet true love is so absent from today's world.

Don't get me wrong. The word "love" is not absent from today's world. It is plastered everywhere you look and used for any number of advertising campaigns, social activism rallies, and political rhetoric. And yet it has become devoid of almost any real substance. Instead of being the most powerful practice in the world, love has been boiled down to half-hearted versions of words like "tolerance" and "fairness" and "equality" and used as a weapon to get what we want. Yet it is so rarely found in the lives of people, even those who would claim the name of Jesus. Consider 1 Corinthians 13:4-7, one of the most concise summaries of the concept of love in Scripture:

> *Love is patient, love is kind. It does not envy, it does not boast, it is not proud. It does not dishonor others, it is not self-seeking, it is not easily angered, it keeps no record of wrongs. Love does not delight in evil but rejoices with the truth. It always protects, always trusts, always hopes, always perseveres.*

Peter calls us to live out love, both to those who are in the church and those who are outside of a relationship with God. If we do, we have the power to change the world.

Think about love like a photo/video program, word processing program, or email program on your computer. Think about how one photo, one video, one story or one email has the power to change the world. Think about how people have taken those photos, videos, or stories and posted them on social media only to find that it goes viral and legitimately changes an aspect of society.

I am sure most of the people that have practiced small acts of love would never think that their simple action would change the world, but so often it does. It might not always be visible or viral, but it is the power of love working through the people of God that can truly bring God's kingdom to earth.

CONCLUSION

This far in the book we have discovered that the source of apathy, depending on our own strength, leads us to depend on our own "promises" and identity instead of God's promises. In this chapter, we discovered that as we start depending on God's power and promises instead of our own, He starts to reboot the practices of our life. Our job is not to change our apathetic practices on our own. Instead, our job is to consistently and intentionally be open to His work in us. As we are open to God changing our practices, He will give us opportunities and strength to add new practices to our life. In the end, our lives will go from apathetic and weak to strong examples of the love of God in the world.

REFLECTION QUESTIONS

1. Do you have a love/hate relationship with technology? Do you feel like it makes your life more effective or less effective?

2. In this chapter, we talked about how we often sabotage our own effectiveness and make ourselves effectively ineffective in the practices of our spiritual life. Have you seen this in your life?

3. One of the reasons we get confused about how to practice our faith is because we have a problem understanding the difference between *being* and *doing*. Some of us feel the need to do more to earn our salvation which is wrong, while others think that everything depends on God and they never take action at all. Do you struggle with seeing the difference between *being* and *doing*?

4. When we first come to know Jesus we are excited to let

God change and update our practices. The further we go in our spiritual walk, the greater the tendency to rationalize away the need to change what we are doing. If you have been in a relationship with Jesus for a while, have you seen this tendency? What is the result of continually dismissing God's calls to take us outside our comfort zone?

5. 2 Peter 1:5-7 says, "For this very reason, make every effort to add to your faith goodness; and to goodness, knowledge; and to knowledge, self-control; and to self-control, perseverance; and to perseverance, godliness; and to godliness, mutual affection; and to mutual affection, love." We talked through each one of these in the chapter. Which one stood out to you the most?

6. Which of the application steps below might be most difficult for you to practice? Why?

APPLICATION

1. BEING AND DOING – If you are someone who is always *doing*, but never *being*, take time to be with God this week. If you are someone who takes a lot of time to *be*, but never takes intentional steps to *do*, then take action this week.

2. PICK A PRACTICE – Pick one of the practices Peter talks about and intentionally ask God to help you grow in that practice this week.

3. HYPOCRISY CHECK – We talked in this chapter how we can become masters at rationalizing away the need to keep growing in our practices. If you read this chapter and thought when you finished, "I am so glad I am doing such a great job at all of these things, and it is a shame that others struggle with them," then I encourage you to stop

and truly ask God to break your heart. I pray each one of us is growing in what we are practicing, but if we are completely sure we have reached the pinnacle of growth then we are being a hypocrite.

Chapter 4

Mental Volatility
REBOOTING THE MEMORY OF OUR SPIRITUAL LIFE

In the first three chapters of this book, the focus has been on how to identify apathy and deal with it in the present. We have looked at the need to reboot the power, promise, and practice of our lives (or the "hardware", "operating system", and "programs" of our lives) in order to deal with apathy and become a passionate follower of Jesus Christ. My prayer is that you have been able to recognize apathy in your own life and find healing from it.

The next three chapters we will look toward setting up a life that is ready to defend against apathy in the future. It is exciting to be free of apathy in the present, but if we are just free for a second and then go right back into it, we will still miss out on becoming a passionate follower of Jesus Christ. In order to set up our lives in a proper way going forward, we will talk about other aspects of our faith that set up the "hardware" and "operating system" and "programs" to be prepared for difficulty.

One of the greatest difficulties facing our lives going forward is "volatility." According to the Merriam-Webster dictionary, the word "volatility" could be described as "a tendency to change quickly and unpredictably."[41] It perfectly describes the tendency for apathy as we look toward the future instead of the past or the present. Life changes, situations change, and relationships change. Yet, it is not only life change that has the power to bring about apathy going forward in our lives. Change is a fact of life but our mental volatility is what is so dangerous.

Growing up, I attended conferences, retreats, and mission trips where the focus was to get away in order to serve people, learn, and spend time with God. Invariably, I would find clarity about God, become passionate about serving Him with all of my heart, and make important decisions about things that needed to look different when I went home. It seemed as if I would never lose the passion I had in those moments. Yet, I remember the warning every youth leader or pastor told us at the end of the trip, "It is going to be easy to forget about this when you get home." At first, I would balk at the idea that something so powerful and passionate as what I was experiencing on the trip would fade so quickly. And yet, without fail, I would watch the tendency in my heart and the heart of others to completely forget the work God did once we arrived home.

I remember coming home from mission trips to Honduras and Haiti where I was confronted with such abject poverty that I was sure my perspective on possessions would never be the same again. In Honduras, we stopped by a landfill area where people were so poor they lived inside the garbage. They would literally build structures inside the landfill and send out their kids, often shoeless, to hunt through the garbage searching for food and other supplies. We visited Haiti after the 2010 major earthquake and everything was devastated. Families were living in tents that heated up to 140 degrees during the day, and they had limited access to the necessities of life.

Coming back from those trips, I felt as though my life would never be the same. Yet, sadly, how volatile our minds and spirits can be. I remember coming back from one of those trips and going straight into a family vacation where we stayed in a friend's gorgeous house on a lake with access to a boat. For the first day or two, I remember feeling so guilty about the disparity between the situation I was currently in and the situation of the people I had just met in Haiti. But after that, it was easy to get wrapped up in the fun we were having and much harder to remember the pain I had just witnessed days before.

Now, I am not saying it is wrong to have fun and enjoy life. I am also not saying it is necessarily wrong to have possessions and money. Our God has given each one of us blessings and gifts to enjoy. What I am saying is that in a world full of fun experiences and flashing lights and impromptu meetings and busy calendars and electronic noise, we have such short attention spans about serious and important matters. This mental volatility is setting us up for apathy.

You see, the work of God can happen in an instant, but He usually chooses to work over a long period of time to shape our lives into what He desires them to be. For instance, imagine a potter at his craft. They have an image of what the pot is going to look like in the end, but it takes a lot of molding and shaping before it becomes what it is meant to be. Now, imagine the potter worked for a couple minutes and took a break, then worked for another couple minutes and got distracted by something else, and so on and so forth. It would take forever for the pot to become what it was meant to be.

Our situation is similar except it is not the potter's fault. If God is the potter and our lives are the clay, He is an ever-present force at work in our lives. He never stops seeking to shape us and mold us into His likeness. The only reason His transforming work would stop in us is if we take ourselves off the potter's wheel. I am concerned that our tendency toward apathy is because we have so much mental volatility or short-term memory issues. God wants to shape our hearts and lives, but we get easily distracted by everyday things and do not leave room or time for God's work to sink in. We experience God's grace, but we don't allow enough room or time for His grace to truly shape us.

We must learn to remember: remember what God has done, remember who we are, and remember what our purpose is. This is our only hope, and this is the next piece of instruction Peter shares with the church in 2 Peter. He talks about the importance of refreshing our memories.

VOLATILE MEMORY

After Peter has finished talking about God's divine power, His great and precious promises, and "making every effort" to add right practices to our lives, he turns his attention to telling the church why he is saying these things to them. He says in 2 Peter 1:12, "So I will always remind you of these things, even though you know them and are firmly established in the truth you now have." He is confident he is talking to people who have heard this message before. Yet, he still feels the need to remind them.

In fact, he says in 2 Peter 1:13, "I think it is right to refresh your memory as long as I live in the tent of this body." He does not feel the need to produce a different message than the one before. Instead, he believes there is power in simply refreshing their memory on a continual basis about the message he has already declared.

His ultimate goal is stated in 2 Peter 1:15, "And I will make every effort to see that after my departure you will always be able to remember these things." His greatest desire is that they would be characterized as a people who could remember the truths of the Gospel on a regular basis. He believes this would keep them from the dangerous teaching of the false teachers and from apathy in their faith.

So why is remembering so important? I think a computer demonstrates this very well. There are two main pieces of hardware in a computer that people refer to as "memory." The first is the hard drive, the long-term storage, where all of your photos, documents, music, and videos are stored so you can go back to them later. A computer can have hundreds, if not thousands, of gigabytes of hard drive space. It functions like our long-term memory.

The other piece of hardware that people call "memory" is RAM or Random Access Memory. This is where data is stored while you are using a particular program. This is more like short-term memory or working memory. Only if something is saved to your computer does it get transferred to your hard drive, or long-term storage.

There are many differences between a hard-drive and RAM. For instance, hard drives can hold more information than RAM, but they are slower to access. RAM is made of semiconductors and hard drives are generally optical or magnetic drives.[42] But the greatest difference between them involves volatility.

Volatile memory is "a memory that loses its contents when the computer or hardware device loses power."[43] RAM is volatile memory whereas a hard-drive is non-volatile memory. So basically, although RAM is the working memory of your computer, if you turn the computer off or reboot the system you will lose everything not saved to the hard-drive.

What does all of this have to do with remembering? Well, imagine, as we have been throughout this book, that we are a computer with hardware, software, and programs running. The hard drive space on our computer would be like our long-term memory, things we do not access all the time, but it is there if we would like to think about it. Included in this would be memories of your growing up years, memories of accomplishments throughout your life, memories of painful circumstances, and memories of relatives and their impact on you. On a normal day, you might not use this memory often unless you are reminiscing or have to think back to something important. We all have many memories that are deep and rich and have really affected who we are today, but rarely do we take the time to reflect on these things.

On a normal day, most of your time is spent using the "RAM" that you have, or your working memory. Your working memory would include details about your presentation at work, where you left your car keys, how many muffins you need to bake for your child to take to her school party, how much money you have left in your bank account, how many appointments you have scheduled for the day, the names of people you are meeting with, and so many other items.

If we are honest, most of us spend the majority of our days

here, and it makes sense; life is busy and there are many things to do. We must give mental energy to remembering these to-do list items or we would not be able to function in life. At the same time, the danger for apathy comes into our lives when the majority of our "RAM" or working memory is only filled up with to-do list items.

Earlier in the book we talked about the danger of having your life be all about "doing" and not about "being." When we start letting our everyday working memory be filled only with to-do list items and never with reflection, the work of God in our lives will start to slow down until it comes to a screeching halt. Why? Because God cares about transforming who we are, not just what we do. And He cannot change who we are unless we stop to let our hearts and minds be open to His transforming work.

Imagine that your life is like a car. You get a brand-new car perfect for long road trips. You enjoy driving and like to get out on the road as often as you can. Every day you keep driving and driving, but you rarely stop for any maintenance. You stop for gas when it is absolutely necessary, maybe getting to within several miles of going completely empty. You may occasionally stop for an oil change, but only after you are over the recommended mileage. You never take the car into the mechanic. You never look at the engine. You never deal with the rust that is starting to form around the body of the car. How long is your car going to last? There comes a point where every single day starts to become dangerous. The chances of a tire going flat, part of your engine failing, or the car falling apart is real possibility.

When we choose every day to let our working memory be filled only with our to-do lists we are putting our hearts and minds in the same danger. For many of us, I think we drive through each and every day with good intentions, but with a dangerous trajectory. We always let our lives get crowded out by what we need to do, not thinking about who we need to become. Just like the car in the example, we can keep pushing our lives to the limit, but some day it will all fall apart. We might be able to handle the occasional bump in the road. But, if we are refusing to allow God to do "maintenance" on our hearts and minds, we will not be able to handle the more difficult situations in life.

This is why so many of us act as though everything is okay in our faith until something truly difficult happens. We do all the right things like going to church and reading our Bibles, but when we get into a situation where a family member is struck with a debilitating disease or a struggle arises within a relationship or we face a difficult time in our job, we feel so weak in our faith. We have not stopped long enough to ask ourselves the most important questions in life. We have not taken enough time to reflect on the grace of God on a daily basis and to remember what He has done for us. We think God has abandoned us, when it is actually the opposite. He has been waiting there the whole time, but slowly and surely we have allowed our hearts and minds to drift from His love and grace.

This is Peter's concern in 2 Peter 1. As Lucas and Green say:

> *The lesson Peter is applying from his own experience is this: no matter how close to the Lord we have been as Christians, or how long-standing our Christian commitment, or how central our position in the fellowship, that danger of wobbling still remains, and we should check ourselves constantly for the tell-tale signs.[44]*

Think about Peter's life. He literally walked around with Jesus. He saw the miracles. He heard the truth. And yet, when the time of testing came he faltered.

As Jesus neared His death on the cross, he told his disciples what was going to happen during the last supper. He tells them it will be a difficult and confusing time and there may be temptation for them to fall away from him. In Matthew 26:33, Peter responds by saying, "Even if all fall away on account of you, I never will." But Jesus says to him in Matthew 26:34, "This very night, before the rooster crows, you will disown me three times." Peter did not believe it. How could he fall away from Jesus? You can imagine him standing up tall and saying, "Even if I have to die with you, I will never disown you."[45] But for anyone who has read this account you know how it ends. As Jesus is arrested and taken away to stand before the religious leaders, Peter denies Jesus not just once, but three times.

Peter knows from personal experience that feeling strong in our own power is so dangerous. He knows that if we are not careful to remember our need for God and how volatile our hearts and minds can be, we are setting ourselves up for apathy and failure. As Lucas and Green say, "The only way to be sure of not wobbling is to remember."[46] The question is: how do we set up our lives in order to remember?

REBOOT YOUR MEMORY

If you have ever been running a lot of programs at the same time on your computer, you may notice that the computer starts to slow down. If it goes on too long, you can even have programs start to quit on you or freeze up. Part of the reason could be that your RAM or working memory is full.[47]

When it gets full, it starts to use virtual memory from the hard drive and this is much slower. One of the easiest solutions in this situation would be to close the programs and reboot your computer. As we talked earlier, this clears out the RAM because it is volatile memory and you can start fresh when you turn the computer back on.

In order to defend against the mental volatility or apathy that comes with living fast-paced lives with little room for reflection, it may be wise to think about how we could continually reboot the working memory of our lives to remember who God is and what He wants to do in our lives.

Remember the Reality of God

In 2 Peter 1:16 through the end of the chapter, Peter seems to change course after talking to the church about refreshing their memory, but what he is really doing is reminding them about the reality of what they believe. He wants them to remember that their faith is based in something real and tangible. He says, "For we did not follow cleverly devised stories when we told you about this coming of our Lord Jesus Christ in power but we were eyewitnesses of his majesty." Peter relates the account of when he and two other disciples stood on the mount of transfiguration and heard God the Father declare Jesus to be His son. He says in 2 Peter 1:18, "We ourselves heard this voice that came from heaven when we were with him on the sacred mountain."

One of the most dangerous aspects of letting our minds constantly be flooded with things we must do and never reflecting is that faith starts to feel disconnected from reality. As Homrighausen says, "It is only by constantly relating our contemporary faith to the norm of revelation events that

Christian experience can be saved from going stale or becoming something less or other than genuinely Christian. Persistent remembrance of these sources of faith is essential to prevent heresy and degeneration."[48] Peter is trying to remind the believers he is speaking to that what Jesus did and said is rooted in reality. Peter had seen and heard the work of God. He can testify that it is real.

So, one of the ways we reboot our working memory on a regular basis is to remember that God is real and active in our lives. We must see and hear the work of God. This might sound simplistic, but it is so important. I am amazed at how many Christians I talk to who can never tell me a time in their life that they have distinctly heard from God or seen God at work. They believe in God, but they do not expect to actually hear from Him and see Him work in their everyday life. Or I talk to many people who have heard from God or seen Him at work, but the last time this happened was five, ten, or fifteen years ago. I always get nervous for those I talk to who never regularly expect to meet with God, because if the circumstances of our life become more real to us than God's ability to work in those situations, we will have such limited faith.

It reminds me of the danger of someone who leaves home to go to college. In college, I was on the leadership team of a freshman dorm. For three years, I watched the reactions of freshman to their new-found freedom. It was interesting to see the difference between those who remembered their parents still existed and those who completely forgot that they had parents. Some people got to school and never went out of their way to contact their parents. It was interesting to see that the less and less their parents became "real" to them, the more unwise decisions they generally made. They were so focused on all the exciting things they could now do at college that they started to forget their parents' wise advice to focus on their studies, get some sleep, and be careful about who they choose as friends. Only when their bank accounts ran empty or everything started to fall apart did they remember they had parents and contact them.

Then there were those who came to school and kept in contact with their parents. They would call on a regular basis, they would ask questions, and they would listen to their parents' advice. They would still have fun and enjoy the freedom they were experiencing, but amid everyday decisions you could tell they were remembering the voice of their parents. Generally, these were the more successful of the freshman, because they did not forget that their parents cared about them and were there for them.

This is somewhat like our relationship with God. When we get so absorbed in our everyday to-do lists and forget that God is alive and active, we start to make unwise decisions. Without even knowing it, a root of apathy starts to grow in our actions, thoughts, and feelings. We stop asking questions like "what would God want in this situation" and "why am I doing what I am doing" and we start asking questions like "how can I get through this day" and "how can I avoid discomfort." We do this because God feels increasingly distant from our daily lives and we wonder whether He can even help anyways.

So how do we remember that God is real and active in our daily lives? One of the primary ways can be summarized by the word "testimony." When we remember the testimony of someone's experience with God or how God showed up in our lives in a powerful way, it grounds us in the reality that God is not a distant God but a present Father. When we see a video of a missionary explaining how God miraculously opened the door for them to share the Gospel with someone or read a book about how God provided for a person in the midst of their darkest time or talk to someone who was transformed from a drug addict into a passionate follower of Jesus, it reboots our memory. It helps us to clear out all the pressure of the to-do lists and reminds us that God can and will meet us in the middle of everyday life.

Whether you know it or not, this is one of the primary goals we should have as we meet in our churches, small groups, and Bible studies. Every time Janelle and I host a small group at our house, we start with a version of the question, "Where have you seen God at work in this past week?" Sometimes there is not much to share, but other times people share amazing testimonies of God's grace. Maybe they saw God work in a conversation that week or bring an answer to a difficult life question or bring healing where it was needed. As each person shares these things in the group, it encourages others that God is still real and active in the world. It clears out the clutter and makes the reality of God's presence tangible.

However, hearing about someone else's experience with God does not sustain us long. At the end of the day, if we constantly hear about God working in other peoples' lives and never experience Him at work in our own, we can start to form a complex. It starts to isolate us even further from God's grace, because we start to imagine something is wrong with us or that other people are just making things up. We might say, "Yes, I believe in God and it is nice that this other person says they are hearing from God, but He does not do that for me. I have to always handle things on my own."

This is why we must not only remember other's testimonies, but remember the testimonies of God working in our own lives. As Homrighausen says:

> *The Christian's mind is a perennial battleground in which memories and ideas and a Presence contend for attention. To forget these things concerning the Lord Jesus Christ — the terms are always used together in II Peter — is to be on the dangerous path that leads to heresy and loss of the faith; to remember continually the things concerning Jesus Christ in ever fresher understanding through the power of the Spirit is to make one's election and calling more certain. Creative remembrance of these things makes for the effective and fruitful knowledge of Jesus Christ (vs. 8). They must be made one's very own through personal appropriation; no second-hand knowledge will suffice. And they must abound through an ever-increasing and continuing meditation and reflection.*[49]

Do you hear what he is saying? If we are to reboot our memory and defend against apathy in our everyday lives, we must remember what is said about God and personally apply it to our everyday life.

This may be as simple as reading 2 Corinthians 5:17 where it says we are now "new creations" in Jesus and remembering how different your life is since you have become a believer in Him. Or it might be remembering how in a simple act of faith the week before, you applied Philippians 4:6-7 to your life and depended on God during a stressful time at work. You may not have realized in the moment, but looking back it is hard to ignore how present God was to bring a coworker through the door at the exact right moment to help you finish that project. Or it might be praising God for being faithful as you watch your long-term prayers answered in the lives of your children.

When we take the time to invite God into our everyday

moments and then praise Him for what He chooses to do, it continually reboots our memory to be concerned about what He wants in our lives and not be just focused on survival. For instance, maybe you are a busy young mom who is stressed out by a thousand different things on a daily basis. Most days you feel like you wander around aimlessly just trying to keep things from falling apart. If you're not careful, you will start losing sight of God's intention for motherhood and spend more of your time complaining about your situation than asking God for guidance. If instead, you start every day with a simple journal, recounting all the blessings from yesterday and in prayer ask God for how He would like you to order your day, you are rebooting your memory and preparing for a new day of motherhood for the Kingdom of God.

Or maybe you are a successful business professional. In the midst of corporate struggles and workplace drama, it can be hard to remember the work and purposes of God. If you are not careful, you will simply fall into the same trap of gossip and drama that everyone else lives in. But, if instead, you take your lunch break to read the Bible and remember the works of God in the lives of Joseph and Nehemiah and Daniel, you will be reminded that God can work in the most interesting ways when we are faithful in positions of power and influence. We will be able to reflect on how God has done that already in our career and also continue to ask Him how we should live that day for His Kingdom.

People ask me all the time how our family kept a passionate relationship with Jesus at the center of our lives as we grew. They think my parents had some special formula or Bible study that if they could just replicate it, it would set their family on the right track. Often to their surprise, they find out there was no special Bible study or formula. The only distinguishing factor about my family compared to other families was that Jesus was invited, talked about, and celebrated all the time in our household.

Dinner times were not just dinner times. It was an opportunity to ask each other how God showed up in our day. Prayer before meals was not just a routine. It was a chance to truly remember that each meal was a blessing from God. Problems at school were not disconnected from the reality of Jesus. The first question my parents would ask or hint at was "how would Jesus want us to handle the drama with our friend or the difficult test or the things that were bringing us anxiety?" What these conversations did was to reboot our memories every day, showing us how Jesus was real and active and that He wanted to shape our lives into something wonderful.

So, if we are to defend against mental volatility or apathy of our everyday thinking, we must remember the reality of God on a regular basis by remembering the testimony of other's lives and the testimony of the working of God in our own lives.

Remember the Truth of God

Even if we remember the testimony of other's lives and our own lives, there is still a chance we will try to do this all in our own strength. What I mean is this: when people say they rely on "positive thinking" or they want to hear more "feel-good stories" in church instead of hard truth, it usually raises red flags in my spirit. Testimony is powerful, but if we are using it as our only source of strength in rebooting our memory then we should be worried. Think of testimony like the sweet dessert at the end of a meal. It is the thing you are most excited to eat and might bring great satisfaction at the end of a meal. But, as we all know, if all we ever ate was dessert, we would be in big trouble. We would be "inflated" with all the calories and it would start to hinder us from doing what we need to do on a daily basis.

This is what happens when people depend solely on stories and "feel-good" experiences to reboot their memory. They might feel an instant jolt, like a sugar rush of a dessert, but no lasting energy from the experience. A consistent struggle with sin comes along or a difficult question they have never thought about comes up, and because they do not have any substance or foundation for why those experiences with God are true they either are forced to ignore the questions or fold under pressure. Either one of these lead to disillusionment and a disconnection from reality again.

We all know we need a balanced diet with some of the less flashy but healthy ingredients as an important part of our diet as well as the desserts. This is why it is so important to listen to what Peter says next about remembering. In 2 Peter 1:19-21 he turns his attention to the "prophetic message" or the Old Testament scriptures. At that time, the New Testament was still being written and had yet to be canonized, but they had access to the story of God in the Old Testament scriptures.

Peter says in verse 19, "We also have the prophetic message as something completely reliable, and you will do well to pay attention to it, as to a light shining in a dark place, until the day dawns and the morning star rises in your hearts." At the time, the false teachers were trying to dissuade the people from believing in the true reality of who Jesus was and what the Christian life was about. Peter says that beyond just the eyewitness testimony he could provide from watching Jesus in person, it was important for the people to trust in and rely on the Scriptures. To help them know they could trust the Scriptures, he explains in verses 20 and 21 that these Scriptures are not just men's opinions. Instead, he says in verse 21, "For prophecy never had its origin in the human will, but prophets, though human, spoke from God as they were carried along by the Holy Spirit." The words of the Bible are the very words of God for our life.

This is why he says the Scriptures are like "a light shining in a dark place." As one commentator says:

> *The main emphasis is manifest: we are on a pilgrimage throughout our lives in this dark world. God has graciously provided us with a lamp, the Scriptures. If we pay attention to them for reproof, warning, guidance, and encouragement we shall walk safely. If we neglect them, we shall be engulfed by darkness. The whole course of our lives ought to be governed by the Word of God.*[50]

Therefore, we must remember the truth of the Bible on a daily basis. This is not just head knowledge. Instead, it is an active remembrance in our daily lives, working itself out in application.

You might say, "Okay, I understand the Bible is important and I try to read a little bit every day. But it does not seem to help me very much." The reason might be very simple. You are simply adding the Bible into your life like you add every to-do list item into your schedule. It is another thing to do. It is weight hanging over you until it is done. Then you get on with your day.

This is not rebooting your memory or remembering. In fact, it is dangerous because you are making the Bible into something it is not – a dead book of knowledge. According to

Hebrews 4:12 the Bible is "alive and active." It is "sharper than any double-edged sword" and "it penetrates even to dividing soul and spirit, joints and marrow; it judges the thoughts and attitudes of the heart." Or as The Message puts it, "His powerful Word is sharp as a surgeon's scalpel, cutting through everything, whether doubt or defense, laying us open to listen and obey."

When we treat the Bible like a dead book of knowledge we think that just by reading it or knowing some facts about it we can find power. But when we understand it is alive and active, we understand that reading it and knowing what it says is important, but more important is reflecting on it for us today. Every time we read Scripture there is the contextual meaning of what it means for the people that it was written to in a specific time and place. It is important that we study the Bible and understand the meaning of what it is saying in context. But it also has a message for us, for this very day. God wants to use it to shape us into who He wants us to be.

In order to let God use His Word to shape our lives, we must consistently and intentionally remember His Word in daily life and meditate on it. A common word picture used in the Bible representing meditating on God's word is a cow chewing its cud.[51] A hungry cow will find a nice patch of grass and start eating. As they eat and start to digest the grass, they will regurgitate it and start chewing it again and again. It might sound a little disgusting, but it is a good illustration of what it means to reflect or meditate on Scripture.

If you get up in the morning and read a passage of Scripture before you head off to work, but do not meditate on it there is a good chance it will do nothing for you. As was said, it is not just about knowing something, it is about receiving something. If instead, you start your time with God by thanking Him for what He has been doing in your life and inviting Him to speak to you as you read the Bible, you set up your heart to meditate. Then, after reading the passage slowly, you do not just rush off but instead start to ask questions about it like "What does this say about God, myself, my life, my family, etc." You spend time in silence, asking God to search your heart and to speak to you about any ways He wants your life to be different because of what you have read. As He guides you, you pray for things that He brings to mind. Then, throughout your day, you look for ways God wants to connect the Truth of His Word to everyday conversations, actions, and thoughts.

Even more beneficial is the practice of taking time to memorize parts of the Bible. This is the ultimate meditation. It takes work and practice for most people to become proficient at memorizing Scripture. But as you do, you start to see how beneficial it is to guard against mental volatility or losing sight of God's purposes in your daily life.

I remember one season of my life when I was struggling with sin and purpose and meaning. I was weighed down with guilt and shame. During that time, it was amazing the power that came from the passages of Scripture I had memorized throughout my life. When I was tempted to despair in guilt or shame and forget about the love and grace of God, I would simply declare the truth of God in the situation. It kept my heart from falling into the trap of apathy and allowed me to be rooted in a place where God's Word could continue to do its work in my heart.

So as much as remembering the reality of God through testimony is an important way to reboot your memory every day, it is also imperative to remember God's Word amid everyday life. As we do this, we will continue to remember we are on a grand adventure with God. There will be ups and downs in the journey, but it will keep our minds and hearts focused on the fact that we cannot stop journeying with God.

CONCLUSION

Dealing with apathy present in our lives is essential and important, but in this chapter we began the discussion about how we need to also defend against apathy in the future. One of the greatest ways to do this is to reboot the working memory of our everyday lives, or the to-do lists and daily things we think about. We reboot our memory by consistently and intentionally remembering the reality of God in everyday life through testimony and remembering the Word of God. In the next chapter, we will discover how to deal with lies and difficulties that come our way.

REFLECTION QUESTIONS

1. In this chapter, the focus was volatility or the "tendency to change quickly and unpredictably." Do you see this tendency in your life?

2. Have you ever experienced God doing something amazing in your life, but within a couple days you forgot about it? Why do you think it was so easy to forget something so powerful?

3. We discovered in this chapter that we must learn to remember: remember what God has done, remember who we are, and remember what our purpose is. Which of these things do you find hardest to remember?

4. We must let God reboot the "working memory" of our lives. If we do not, it is like a car that keeps being driven without any maintenance. At some point, it is going to fall

apart. Have you ever had a time in your life when things came crashing down around you and you did not have the strength of faith to face it?

5. One of the greatest ways to reboot the memory of your life is to remember the reality of God. This happens by hearing the testimony of other people or remembering the testimony of what God has done in your own life. When was a time that you heard a testimony and it encouraged you to remember the reality of God? How can you more actively hear and also share testimony in your life?

6. Another way to reboot the memory of your life is to remember the Truth of God. Meditating on Scripture and memorization of Scripture are two powerful ways to remember the Truth of God. What are some ways you can better practice these in your life?

7. Which of the application steps below might be most difficult for you to practice? Why?

APPLICATION

1. RECOGNIZE MENTAL VOLATILITY – We cannot deal with mental volatility until we recognize it. Pray and ask God to give you a sensitivity to when you forget His presence in your life.

2. REMEMBER THE REALITY OF GOD – If you have never done this, start to ask the question, "Where has God shown up today (or this week)" in your family on a regular basis or in your group of friends on a regular basis.

3. REMEMBER THE TRUTH OF GOD – Start to meditate on and memorize Scripture. Talk to someone further along the journey about some ways to do this or look online for some helpful resources.

Chapter 5

Firewall Free Fall
REBOOTING DISCERNMENT IN OUR SPIRITUAL LIFE

My college dormitory had an open-door policy for those who were leaders. Basically, if we were present in the dorm, we were expected to have our door physically open so that anyone could come in at any time. I completely understood the reasoning behind the policy. The dorm housed freshman and the hope was that by having our doors open, hesitant freshman would know there was always someone available who could answer questions or provide support.

Even though I understood the policy, it did not mean it was easy for me to practice. Anyone could wander in at any time with any set of issues and I had to help them while still trying to finish my own school work. I remember having to counsel stressed freshman who were concerned that they might have to pull an all-nighter to write a two-page paper while I was trying to finish my own fifteen-page paper before I went to bed. I was happy to help, but it was not easy to balance it all.

Beyond that, there was something fundamentally disconcerting about never getting to close your door. There is something deep within us that desires limits. We desire closure and protection from unwanted influences or distractions. We desire to have some sort of control over the random chaos that could overtake us.

Look at our desire to build walls, lock doors, buy safes, and use other forms of security. Even the most freewheeling person among us has their limits. We understand deep down that not every force or person is a good one, and we know we must protect the things in our lives from those dangerous forces. So, we build walls. We lock our doors. We make back-ups of important documents. We make emergency plans. We avoid the open-door policy in our lives because we know the damage that can come from refusing to discern between good and bad forces.

Yet, I am continually shocked how infrequently we consider the same kind of protection for our minds and hearts. We might go to extravagant steps to protect our finances or our homes or our computers, but we do not put the same kind of effort into protecting the very heart of who we are. Instead, we live in this depressing and destructive cycle of apathy resulting from what I call "firewall free fall."

In the technology world, a firewall is "a software program or piece of hardware that helps screen out hackers, viruses, and worms that try to reach your computer over the Internet."[52] As computers were developed, it became clear that hackers could exploit certain doorways into a computer to steal information and resources. It was necessary to develop a filtering system to stop destructive attacks while allowing other information to continue flowing to the computer, so firewalls were developed for business and home computers. If a computer does not have a strong firewall, it is constantly left open to malicious attacks, called malware, that may do many destructive things like steal important information, delete essential programs, or take over control of your computer.

In a similar way, if our hearts and minds do not have a strong "firewall," we can leave ourselves open to destructive lies and half-truths leading us straight back to apathy. Remember, in the first half of the book we talked about ways to deal with apathy present in our lives. In this second half of the book, we are focusing on ways to defend against apathy in the future; and rebooting discernment in our spiritual life is essential to that goal. If we do not have a way of filtering out lies from truth in what we hear and see every day, we will live life in a constant free fall. We may occasionally receive some truth from God bringing freedom from our apathetic free fall for a moment, but it will be the natural pattern of our lives to fall back into apathy.

Honestly, this free fall is where so many of us live, but it is hard for us to understand why we feel the way we do. People use different words to describe what they are feeling. Some Christians say, "I want to believe in God entirely, but I still have doubts. I probably always will, though, so I guess I will have to deal with it." Others say, "We are all broken, aren't we? There's nothing you can really do about it until we get to heaven." Still others say, "I believe in the Bible, but almost all religions have some of the same tenets. We just have to try to live a good life following the golden rule." And one of the more dangerous responses is, "I do not want to look differently from the world around me because then people will not want to follow Jesus. They might think I am strange if I am too 'holy' so I want to make sure that I am still watching the same things, listening to the same things, and doing the same things they do."

These are honest thoughts and feelings, but they are lies or half-truths. They are attitudes to be dealt with, but we treat them like guiding principles. Remember when we talked about fundamental promises in chapter two? Instead of depending on the fundamental promises of God, we follow these "promises." And because we have not developed or practiced a way to discern between lies and truth, we always revert to our apathetic free fall.

We might hear a powerful sermon that addresses one of the major doubts we have, but the next time a different doubt comes our way we revert to the apathy of not really trusting God with our lives. We might see transformation in our lives as we pray and ask God to help us overcome a sin issue, but the next time we pray and nothing seems to happen we revert to the apathetic position of assuming we are just going to be broken until we die. We might have a friend help us realize destructive patterns in our lives have occurred because we are trying to look too much like the world, but the fear of being different keeps us from submitting that destructive pattern to the Lord.

You see, if we are not clear on the truth, then we cannot clearly discern what is right and wrong. And if what we know and what we experience never align, we will always return to apathy. We must understand how deception can lead us to apathy and how to reboot the "firewall" of our lives. In the second chapter of 2 Peter, Peter begins teaching on the destructive nature of lies and how to deal with them.

THREE PRINCIPLES OF LIES

Peter begins with a dire truth in verse one of 2 Peter 2: "But there were also false prophets among the people, just as there will be false teachers among you." His point is that we must be careful about who and what we listen to. In his day, "teachers occupied a very high place in the early church, bracketed with prophets as possessing one of the esteemed higher gifts."[53] Unfortunately, some of those who were teaching in the church were spreading falsehood. Instead of teaching the truth, Peter warns that these teachers sought to "secretly introduce destructive heresies" into the church.[54] Or as The Message version of 2 Peter 2:1 says, "They'll smuggle in destructive divisions, pitting you against each other."

Peter's primary concern in 2 Peter 2 is to help the believers understand that there is a constant need for discernment, even within the church. His concern focused primarily on these false teachers who were promoting dangerous heresies like the lie that Jesus was not returning as He had promised. But if we were to apply his directives in a wider circle, we can start to see a pattern emerging for what happens in our lives when we choose not to discern between truth and lies. There are three principles we must understand about lies if we are to defend against them.

PRINCIPLE 1 – Good Lies are Hard to Detect

The first principle is that the most dangerous and destructive lies are not blatant. Even the least discerning among us can usually detect blatant lies. When my nephew was almost two years old, he was told one day to stay away from the Christmas ornaments on their tree. My sister walked into the room the tree was in and found him touching a Christmas ornament. She asked him if he was disobeying and with his hand still on the ornament, he confidently said "no." If you are a parent, you have probably encountered your young children in this same predicament. They have not yet learned that blatant lies do not work because they are so obvious.

I believe many of us think that lies in our spiritual lives will be as easy to detect as the lies that our kids might tell. Unfortunately, most of the lies that surround us daily are dangerous half-truths. We must be most vigilant to detect half-truths. Peter discusses the dangerous nature of lies and half-truths as he describes the false teachers in 2 Peter 2. He acknowledges how the false teachers know they cannot offer blatant lies to the Christians. Instead, they "secretly" introduce the lies. There is intention behind what they are doing. They are trying to package the lie in something more palatable.

One of the ways lies are smuggled into our lives is through stories. Peter says the false teachers would use "fabricated stories" to get their lies across. Lucas and Green say of these stories, "They might be stories about the impressiveness of their ministry or about new truths that God has taught them, but the stinging condemnation is that they have made them up."[55] The intention of the false teachers was to use a false story to bypass any doubts the people may have about the content of what they were saying. They were hoping the people may say, "I am not sure that what they are saying is correct, but if their ministry is thriving or if it sounds good enough it must be true." Stories, if used intentionally as weapons, can be so dangerous because they bypass the mind and go directly to the emotions.

Anthony Tjan, speaking from the perspective of a venture capitalist, says in his article *The Indispensable Power of Story*,

"Heart, guts, and the ability to connect are critical in the early stages of company creation and beyond. The durability or effectiveness of any leadership or partnership requires this ability to connect and share a story — people need to just feel it."[56] His last statement summarizes the power of stories well: "People need to just feel it."

In this post-modern world, society is much less concerned about the truth of something and much more concerned with how it feels. Just look at any form of social media. There is a reason pictures and videos and stories perform much better on social media than articles or arguments. Advertisers and content creators know that if they can touch the hearts of people through story and make them feel something, they are much more likely to accept the message behind it.

I am not trying to say that all stories are bad and we should live in a sterile, emotionless environment where everything is based on logic and reason. In fact, I think stories can be a powerful tool in the hands of Christians and churches. Jesus consistently used parables and stories to communicate the Truth. What I am saying, though, is that if someone is trying to deceive you, they are likely to package it in a story so it is harder to detect.

It reminds me of phishing – one of the ways hackers try to gain access to a computer. Phishing is "a form of fraud in which an attacker masquerades as a reputable entity and person in email or other communication channels."[57] You have probably seen these kinds of emails before. You get a message that appears to be from someone you know or a company you use, but they are asking you to fill in your personal information or follow a link. If you were to proceed to fill in your information or click on the link, the hackers would have a wide-open door to steal from you or attack your computer in another way.

Now, if you are discerning in reading your emails, it is pretty easy to spot these phishing attacks. Typically, the links or the company name are spelled wrong or the imagery used might seem a bit off. Or it might just sound differently than how the person or company normally speaks. However, many people are victims of phishing attacks daily.

Why? The reason these attacks are so deceptive is because they are wrapped in a story of sorts. If you were to get an email from a hacker directly asking you for money you would immediately delete it. That would be too blatant. But when they wrap their message up and pretend to be someone you know there is a story behind it. There is emotion attached to it. In fact, in a certain kind of phishing attack the hackers impersonate someone in need from another country to pull on the listener's heart strings. Their intention is to try to blind you with a story so you cannot see the lie.

Whether it is through stories, like the false teachers used, or another means, good lies are hard to detect. The most dangerous form of lies are half-truths: lies that use a little bit of the truth to anesthetize us to the reality of the falsehood behind it. The earliest example comes from the prince of lies himself, Satan. In Genesis 2:16-17, we see God set Adam in the garden and put this one restriction on him, "And the Lord commanded the man, "You are free to eat from any tree in the garden; but you must not eat from the tree of the knowledge of good and evil, for when you eat from it you will certainly die.""

In Genesis 3, the serpent (or Satan) comes to Eve to deceive her into disobeying God. He could have blatantly lied, but he knew that would not work. So, he utilized a half-truth. He said to Eve in Genesis 3:1, "Did God really say, 'You must not eat from any tree in the garden?'" Now, the truth is that God did ask them to not eat from one particular tree in the garden, but they were allowed to eat from any other tree. Satan used this one true aspect, God asking them not to eat from one particular tree, in order to craft a lie that made God seem selfish and unconcerned about Adam and Eve's needs.

You can tell that the lie is having its intended effect when Eve responds in Genesis 3:3, "We may eat fruit from the trees in the garden, but God did say, 'You must not eat fruit from the tree that is in the middle of the garden, and you must not touch it, or you will die.'" Do you see what happened? She tries to speak the truth of what God said, but she adds something that God did not say. She adds they must not even touch the tree. God did not say this, and in some ways it makes Him sound more restrictive than He actually was. The lie is starting to do its work of confusion.

Finally, Satan goes in with the second and final half-truth. Genesis 3:4 says, "'You will not certainly die,' the serpent said to the woman. 'For God knows that when you eat from it your eyes will be opened, and you will be like God, knowing good from evil.'" Is this true? Well, it is partially true. God does know that their eyes will be opened when they eat from the tree, but it will not be a blessing. When they finally take the fruit and eat it, they realize they are naked and become ashamed and fearful. God is trying to protect Adam and Eve, but Satan uses half-truths to get them to doubt the character of God Himself.

This is what Satan still does today. John 10:10 says, "The thief (Satan) comes only to steal and kill and destroy." John 8:44 says, "You belong to your father, the devil, and you want to carry out your father's desires. He was a murderer from the beginning, not holding to the truth, for there is no truth in him. When he lies, he speaks his native language, for he is a liar and the father of lies." His intention in our lives is to deceive us from living a passionate life for God. He knows he cannot do it directly, so he works behind the scenes to deceive us with half-truths.

There is no greater book at showing the danger of the enemy's half-truths than C.S. Lewis' book *The Screwtape Letters*. In this book, he details the communication taking place between a fictional demon, Screwtape, and his nephew, Wormwood, who is being trained in the ways of tempting.[58] In these letters, they refer to God as the "enemy" and discuss how the temptation of a particular human is progressing. Lewis' masterful work in these conversations brings clarity to the danger of half-truths in our lives.

For instance, at one point in their conversations Screwtape says, "If you can once get him to the point of thinking that 'religion is all very well up to a point,' you can feel quite happy about his soul. A moderated religion is as good for us as no religion at all - and more amusing."[59] Do you see the intention behind this? Lewis' point is that Satan does not always try to blatantly tempt us to abandon faith. He would just as likely try to use half-truths and rationalizations to get us to a "moderated religion" or a spiritual journey under our own power and control and promises. From what we have discussed in the book so far, we know that depending on our own power and promises simply leads to apathy. Satan would love nothing more than to use good half-truths to lead us back to apathy.

At another point in "The Screwtape Letters," Screwtape says, "The more often he (the person being tempted) feels without acting, the less he will be able ever to act, and, in the long run, the less he will be able to feel."[60] Again, this shows the power of half-truth. The enemy's intention was to get the person to feel something without doing anything about it. A modern example might be the supposed power of the hashtag. Every time there is a significant news story, people fly to social media to duke it out, using hashtags as their weapons of choice. Yet, at the end of the day, you might hashtag your support for something without ever doing anything tangible about it.

For instance, you may put up a hashtag about racial division and yet never actually act to love people of other races in a more intentional way in your life. You think a hashtag somehow made you part of the fight. But if you only ever respond to issues with a hashtag you will increasingly find yourself less likely to do or feel much about anything.

Good lies are hard to detect and we must be careful to realize that when it comes to our hearts and minds, we are up against the very prince of lies himself, Satan. Whether through stories or half-truths, the lies that can damage our very souls are not always easy to see.

PRINCIPLE 2 – Lies Appeal to Our Pride

The second principle regarding lies connects with the first. Another reason good lies are hard to detect is not only because of how they are communicated, but how they appeal to our pride. This becomes very clear as we listen to Peter's examination of the false teachers' lies. He says in 2 Peter 2:1 that they "secretly introduce destructive heresies, even denying the sovereign Lord who bought them." Lucas and Green say,

These words would have an extraordinary poignancy for Peter as he wrote them. He knew the shame of denying Jesus, even though Jesus

had foretold it; and he knew the humble wonder of being restored. But where Peter had known a spasm of cowardice, these men were settled in their opposition and showed no inclination to remorse or forgiveness.[61]

The appeal of the false teachers' lies would have been freedom. Freedom to make their own decisions. Freedom to choose what kind of lifestyle they wanted to live. Freedom to hold God at arm's length so that although they believed in Him, they could also decide which of His standards to obey.

This falls in line with the second principle behind almost every lie: Good lies appeal to our pride and control. At the end of the day, pride is the root of all sin. When we sin, we are choosing to take our life into our own hands and rebel against the ways of God. Part of what made the lies of the false teachers so destructive is that they denied the rightful place of God in peoples' lives, but that is also what made them so deceptive. Whether we want to admit it or not, we like it when things are under our control.

When my sister went to take her permit test to start driving, she failed the test. I felt bad for her but at the same time, I said to myself, "This is a small test and if they would only give me a chance to take it I am sure I would have passed." A couple years later, my turn came around. I walked in with a smirk on my face, thinking that I was going to ace this measly test and show my sister how easy it was. Imagine my surprise when I failed. I thought that if given the right opportunity, I had the power to do better than my sister. Obviously, that was not true.

This is the kind of attitude we so often have with God. We see where our life is heading and we honestly start to think that God is doing a pretty bad job of being in control of our life. We feel as though we are doing what He has asked of us and yet painful things keep happening, our dreams are not becoming a reality, and we feel like life should be different. Imagine the temptation that comes with a lie that puts us in control and denies God's rightful place in our lives. Even though we always fail, just like I did with my permit test, we still continue to imagine that life might be better under our own control.

One of the ways lies appeal to our pride is to convince us we need not submit to authority. Peter says of the false teachers in 2 Peter 2:10 that they "despise authority" and are "bold and arrogant." Because of this arrogance, he says in 2:12 that they "blaspheme in matters they do not understand." They did not want anyone to have authority over them and the lies they spread would have appealed to this sinful attitude in others.

A person that is unfettered from any authority is a dangerous person and yet we, as a society, celebrate independence from authority daily. Instead of celebrating when someone abides by the law, people rationalize why certain people should have the right to break the law. Some even go so far as to celebrate when they do it. Instead of standing up for the right of the employer to hold a certain standard, society likes to stand up for the underdog and fight against "the man." Now, I am not making a political statement, because in talking about politics or government or corporations there could be endless discussions about corrupt systems and corrupt people. What I am trying to point out is how quickly we are willing to celebrate with someone who throws off the yoke of obedience and submission.

In our spiritual lives, Satan would love nothing more than to convince us that we do not need authority in our lives. An effective lie leads us to the place of throwing off the authority of God, our parents, our pastors, and other influential people. I could give you countless examples of this from my time as a pastor. I remember one circumstance when a girl came to visit our college ministry for the first time. She had come because of the radio spots we had on a secular radio station. She was a nice girl, but it became obvious very quickly that she was stuck in a pattern of sin. The girls in her small group loved her and sought to share the truth of the Gospel with her. She said she loved being there with us.

After she had attended the group for a while, she talked to me about a particular issue in her family. As I listened, it was evident to me that part of the overlying issue was the fact that she did not want anyone to have authority over her decisions and her life. I gently talked about needing to surrender control of every part of her life to God when she came to Him, even the sinful patterns she was living out. She immediately got angry and left. We tried to reach out to her, but she never returned. She did apologize at one point, however, realizing how emotionally she had reacted. What she did not understand, unfortunately, is that the reason she reacted so powerfully to my gentle suggestion is because she was believing a lie that appealed to her desire to not submit to any authority.

The other way lies appeal to our pride is to affirm in us a "freedom for self-expression."[62] The false teachers of Peter's day were living lives full of greed and lust. In 2 Peter 2:13-14 it says, "Their idea of pleasure is to carouse in broad daylight. They are blots and blemishes, reveling in their pleasures while they feast with you. With eyes full of adultery, they never stop sinning; they seduce the unstable; they are experts in greed – an accursed brood." They wanted to freely express themselves in how they acted, what they thought about, and how they felt about the world around them. In fact, they felt like it was their right.

I am not sure if something could be more applicable in today's culture and climate. This is the battle cry of almost every song, movie, advertisement, self-help book, and college campus. Certain phrases like "I just need to be me" and "don't let anyone change you" have become so much a part of our vernacular that they are almost cliché. Every song or anthem promotes throwing off restraint and living for today. The hero of almost every movie only needs a chance to truly express themselves and then they succeed. Every self-help book tells you that if anyone holds you back from expressing your mind then they are your enemy.

College campuses take it to another level when they open doors of self-expression for students that seem almost absurd. Safe spaces and trigger warnings and similar ideas can so easily be dangerous, half-truth lies that hinder people from finding freedom by containing them within a bubble of their own self-expression and self-pity. Some students at the University of Oregon were so worried about self-expression that they considered taking down a poster from the hallway featuring a quote from Martin Luther King Jr's "I Have a Dream" speech. They said that it was not inclusive enough, fearing that it might offend some people who were not included.[63]

A student at Edinburgh University in Scotland apparently violated the school's "safe space policy" by raising her hand in disagreement during a student council meeting. According to Katherine Timpf, the school's safe space policy "strictly forbade 'hand gestures which denote disagreement' because apparently they are just too scary for adult students to handle."[64]

You might say, "Well, this sounds like it limits self-expression instead of opening up doors for self-expression."

119

But that is the rub. When you promote self-expression to such an extent that everyone has the right to express themselves in every way they deem right, the only thing that is considered wrong is trampling on someone else's self-expression.

If you read the news today or listen to the chatter in your office at work, people have thrown off "old-fashioned" restraints of abstinence from things like alcohol, sex, and drugs. They have rebelled against "old-fashioned" institutions like marriage and the church. In fact, if you are someone who for the sake of God abstains from sex before marriage, does not participate in drugs and alcohol, looks forward to marriage and family, and loves the church you are treated like a mythical beast or something. This was my experience growing up. People looked at me like I had a third eye because I stood for what they considered "old-fashioned" restraints of morality.

Most people are willing to disregard these "old-fashioned" restraints without so much as a thought and they might make fun of someone that holds to this lifestyle. The only thing that you dare not trample on in society today is "self-expression." The reason why this is so powerful and important to so many people is because they have numerous lies based on self-expression holding up their life.

They believe deep down there is no one else they can trust with their life. They also believe their happiness and satisfaction is the most important objective in life. To achieve that happiness, they believe they must have free and unfettered autonomy in their morality, their expression, and their decisions. They believe that attaining sexual satisfaction, entertainment, and comfort by whatever means they choose is their right.

I keep saying "they," but what I really should be saying is "we." You might say, "I do not live without restraints. I try to follow after God and His desires for me." I understand. I think most of us who are followers of Jesus do honestly try to follow Him. What concerns me is this same principle of lies appealing to our pride that is demonstrated in society can impact us in the same way, even if it is not as overt.

For instance, you might be trying to live a pure life by following God's commands on sexual satisfaction, all the while having no qualms about watching explicit scenes in R-rated movies. Or you might not go out and get drunk every night, but you get perturbed when someone questions whether the way you are using your free time is distracting you from the mission of God. Or you might mock others for desiring "safe spaces," all the while being terrified to share your testimony with someone else. Self-righteousness, or feeling good about who you are in comparison to another, is a dangerous lie in terms of apathy. It looks different, but it follows the exact same principle of appealing to our pride.

PRINCIPLE 3 – Lies Bring Destruction

This third principle is less about the content of lies and more about identifying lies by their result. In 2 Peter 2:1, Peter says these false teachers who are introducing heresies and denying the sovereign Lord are "bringing swift destruction on themselves." Later on, he uses two images to demonstrate the kind of destruction they bring not only on themselves, but on others.

First, Peter says they are "springs without water."[65] In the following verse he says, "For they mouth empty, boastful words and, by appealing to the lustful desires of the flesh, they entice people who are just escaping from those who live in error."[66] Of these false teachers it has been said, "Overblown, with exaggerated claims dressed in fancy words, these people were like spiritual puffer fish, inflating themselves to impress and intimidate."[67]

The claims of the lies seeking entrance into our lives are big and bold. We are tempted by them because they seem to promise satisfaction in ways we do not currently feel satisfied. These are lies like, "If I take over control of my life from God at least I will feel safe" or "if I flirt with that person at work it won't hurt anyone" or "if I just buy this one last thing I will be satisfied" or "if I can just sacrifice time with God and my family for a little while to get that job promotion it will all be worth it."

However, one of the ways that lies and sin destroy us is by promising fulfillment, but ultimately making us less fulfilled than we were before. They are dry springs, a place where you would think water would be flowing, but it is bone dry. My wife mocks me because I do not like to go anywhere without a water bottle. The other day she was laughing because we were running into an appointment for less than ten minutes and I took my water bottle with me. I am pretty sure I did not even drink any water while we were there and it is an awkward thing to have to carry around. The reason I always carry a water bottle with me, though, is because I get hyper when I get extremely thirsty and have no access to water. So, this idea of a dry spring carries extra weight for me.

Imagine you are walking through a seemingly endless desert and you come upon what looks like a well. You run to the well as quick as you can get there, lower the bucket down to get water, and all you hear at the bottom is hard ground. This is one of the ways that lies destroy us. They continually take from us instead of giving. They leave us unfulfilled, broken, and stumbling through life. In Jeremiah 2:13, God describes the situation like this, "My people...have forsaken me, the spring of living water, and have dug their own cisterns, broken cisterns that cannot hold water."

This must have been the predicament of the woman at the well in John 4. Jesus starts speaking with the Samaritan woman in John 4:7 and asks her for a drink of water. Throughout the conversation you can see the evidence of several lies as she seeks to deflect the conversation in different directions. In some ways, she is probably embarrassed and disappointed in the "dryness" of her life. Jesus finally confronts her with the truth that he knows she has had five husbands and is living with another guy. Obviously, the destructive nature of lies has taken its toll on her life.

Jesus offers her the only hope she has, "But whoever drinks the water I give them will never thirst. Indeed, the water I give them will become in them a spring of water welling up to eternal life."[68] But for many of us, we simply continue the free fall of destruction, pursuing the emptiness that comes from following lies.

Driven Mists

The other picture Peter uses to talk about the destructive nature of lies is "mists driven by a storm."[69] Peter understood what it was like to be in a storm as he had "encountered storms on the sea of Galilee, and knew the powerlessness the crew of a small boat feel in the face of such strong gales."[70] Mist has no power in and of itself. It is driven along by some other force.

In the same way, lies promise independence and empowerment. They promise a sense of control. And yet, the destructive nature of lies is that they disempower us. As Peter

123

says in 2 Peter 2:19, "They (the false teachers) promise them freedom, while they themselves are slaves of depravity – for people are slaves to whatever has mastered them."

You might say, "Well, I will never let myself be mastered by anything." And I would say you have already been destroyed by a lie – a lie that you are in control. The Bible makes it clear that "no-one is without a master, and if the false teachers do not serve Christ as his slaves, then, by definition, they serve sin and its master."[71] Or, as another commentator says, "In a sense, there are only two religions in the world: one is a human system by which man seeks to make himself acceptable to God; and the other is that divine action by which God has provided man with justification and reconciliation. One is of man, the other of God."[72]

What we must realize is that every day there is a reason behind everything we do, whether we know it or not. Every action you take and every thought you think from the moment you wake until the time you go to sleep is based on what you believe. As Homrighausen says, "What a person believes is of utmost importance, for it determines his attitude and his conduct. Right thoughts precede right actions; they determine the release of the emotions. They express themselves in social relation, in daily work, and in the life of the home."[73] If the beliefs of our lives are true, then the fruit of our life will be right actions and right conduct.

Yet, when we choose to believe lies, their destructive nature produces a powerlessness to our lives. Since the lies become the foundation of our beliefs, the actions and thoughts of our life follow the same direction. Relate this to our example of a computer virus. Some computer viruses infect a computer and take control of the computer itself. Everything the computer does is now under the control of another person.

Remember, in chapter two how we talked about God being the root user, or person in control, of the operating system of our lives? The choice really comes down to this – do we want God to be in control of our operating system or are we allowing the destructive nature of lies to make us submit to their power?

I have seen many real-life examples of this in the prayer counseling sessions we host at the church. I have done this type of prayer counseling with well over a hundred people now. In these sessions, we have a guided conversation where we ask God to enlighten the person seeking counsel to where lie-based belief might be in their lives. When we find these beliefs, we then direct them to pray over those lies and ask God to give them the truth about the situation.

Lies come from many different sources in these sessions, but the emotion attached to these sources is pain. When we experience pain, whether it is pain from our childhood or a traumatic experience later in life, we often are faced with a choice: will we bring that pain to God or will we keep that pain to ourselves and allow it to develop into a lie? If believed consistently over time, these lies can be so destructive to everyday life.

For instance, many times the lie boils down to a sense that God cannot be trusted. The person comes into a session with constant anxiety, a sense that they need to be in control of every person and every situation in their life, and a bad track record of letting their anger destroy people around them. Now that I have facilitated so many sessions and I understand better how our beliefs determine our actions and thoughts, it becomes obvious very quickly when people are living out the destructive nature of the lie that God cannot be trusted.

Because they experienced something terrible and they chose to deny that God was present in their situation, without even knowing it every part of their life has been taken into their control. They may still go to church and volunteer and try to read their Bible every day, but they are not doing it in the strength of God or trusting God. They are doing it because they believe it is the right thing to do and they have to do the right things perfectly because they believe all of life depends on them. No wonder they are suffering with anxiety, control, and anger issues.

When we choose to believe lies, we are like "mists driven by a storm," unable to fight back against the overwhelming force and weight of the lies we believe. And none of us is exempt. I have actually found that some of the hardest people to do the prayer counseling sessions with are those that have been Christians the longest. It is easy for someone who has not learned much about God to acknowledge they might be living out lies. It is not always as easy for a long-term Christian who thinks they are doing all the right things to acknowledge that destructive lies are present in their life.

We must remember the three principles of lies we have learned, though. First, good lies are hard to detect. Second, lies appeal to our pride. Finally, lies bring destruction. So what hope do we have in this world full of lies? How do we prepare ourselves so we are less likely to fall into a pattern of returning to apathy?

HOW TO DEVELOP A FIREWALL

In order to be prepared to face the onslaught of lies surrounding us, we must develop a spiritual firewall. Remember, we talked earlier how firewalls help to discern between what should enter a computer system and what should be blocked. We must consistently and intentionally develop some of the same patterns in our spiritual lives. We must become rooted in the truth so we can stand against any lies that come our way.

Become Aware

The first and simplest way we can develop a spiritual firewall is to become aware. For many of us, we do not normally think on this level on a regular basis. You might say, "Honestly, Justin, this stuff seems a little deep and I am just trying to get through each day the best I can." I understand where you are coming from. We live busy lives with many family, work, and social responsibilities. But going back to what I said at the beginning of the chapter, despite our busy schedules we still take time and effort to secure the things most precious to us. We still make an effort to lock our doors and to secure our computers, and we do that without any knowledge of an attack coming against us.

The reality is whether you want to believe it or not, you are most certainly under attack from a spiritual perspective. Everything you hear, see, and experience is delivering a message or a worldview. When you listen to the radio on the way to work, it is not just news. It is news with a worldview. When you have a conversation with someone at work or a coffee shop, it is not just conversation. It is conversation with a worldview behind it. When you watch that YouTube video, listen to that song, and watch that movie they all have an underlying message and worldview behind them. I do not say this to make you terrified to do anything.

What I am saying is that we must become aware that everything we hear, see, and experience has the potential to be communicating a lie to us. If we are aware of this, then we can start to practice discernment.

Become Discerning

Discernment is "nothing more than the ability to decide between truth and error, right and wrong." Or put another way it is "the ability to think with discernment is synonymous with an ability to think biblically."[74] God calls us to become discerning within our everyday lives. In 1 Thessalonians 5:20-22 it says, "Do not treat prophecies with contempt but test them all; hold on to what is good, reject every kind of evil." In 1 John 4:1 it says, "Dear friends, do not believe every spirit, but test the spirits to see whether they are from God, because many false prophets have gone out into the world." We must learn to become discerning of the messages we hear every day.

According to the Scriptures quoted above we are to test prophecies and things we hear. Other passages in Scripture including 2 Corinthians 13:5 and Galatians 6:4 talk about testing ourselves and our actions. Romans 12:2 talks about testing and approving God's will, in the sense that as our minds are transformed to look more like Him, we will better understand how to live and act. In 1 Timothy 3:10, we are called to test those who are put forth as leaders in the church. If we are going to have any hope of avoiding the "Firewall Free Fall," we must make it a practice to discern in every situation.

The best way to accomplish this is to always ask questions. Parents often joke about that age where your child becomes old enough to start asking questions. The questions start slowly, but once a child gets started they never stop. Questions like "why is the sky blue" and "why do I need to wear shoes" and "why are frogs slimy" become the norm. Most parents dread this age, but when we had our son Judah, I was actually looking forward to it. In fact, I think young children have an attitude that we need to rediscover in our adult lives. To them, everything is new. They are constantly testing the world around them, excited about what they will find. Sometimes, it is nothing extraordinary. Other times, what they learn astonishes them.

We must rediscover the power of questions. In our case, we must understand that when we have a fight with our spouse, it is not just a fight. There is something behind that fight. When we are constantly on the edge financially and we cannot seem to stop spending money, it is not just a lack of a higher paying job. There is something behind that spending. When we judge the world around us and choose not to love certain people we encounter, it is not just "the way that person is." There is something behind that lack of love. Questions have the power to unlock the answers to what is causing issues in our lives.

The main question we must ask of anything we are receiving is, "Is this true?" Remember, we said that good lies are hard to detect. This is why it is important that we pass anything we hear through several layers of testing to see if it is true. The Wesleyan quadrilateral, named after John Wesley, gives a powerful way of discerning truth. The four elements of the quadrilateral are scripture, reason, faith, and experience. Each one of these layers helps us to discern the truth of something.

The most important element is Scripture. When we encounter anything including a worldview, a difficult situation, or a form of entertainment we should ask the question, "What would the Bible say about this?" In fact, even when we encounter feelings we have about a certain situation or person in our life we should ask, "Would the Bible say this is true or right?" For instance, say your spouse did something to you that was really hurtful and you feel justified in believing you deserve better from them. Because of this belief you start yelling at them and treating them with disrespect. The first question we should ask is, "Would the Bible say it is true and right for me to feel this way about my spouse?"

The second element of the quadrilateral is reason: "Does this make sense?" Another way of asking this could be, "Is this wise?" This is often tied together with the Bible. For instance, you might say, "The Bible never talks about playing video games or watching TV or surfing Facebook. Therefore, I am off the hook and can make a decision about what is best in those situations." But the Bible talks a lot about how we use our time, our energy, and our minds. Asking the question, "Does this make sense" or "is this wise" helps to determine what is true and right in this case.

The third element of the quadrilateral is tradition: "Historically, how have Christians viewed this?" In everyday life, I think the best way to practice this is to ask wiser and older Christians about things we are going through. For instance, say you are a young believer who has been dating a boyfriend or girlfriend for a while and things are getting serious. Most of your coworkers are confused why you have not moved in together or slept together. Maybe you have researched Scripture and think you found some answers, but you are not quite sure how to figure out exactly what it is saying. This is a great chance to find someone who is farther along the journey in their spiritual life and ask them. You could ask, "What does the Bible say about purity" or "how has the church dealt with purity in the past."

The final element is experience. This one needs some explanation. I have talked to so many people over the years who when I ask them why they did something, say, "I asked God and He gave me a sign." Now, I do not doubt that God gives signs to us sometimes about certain situations, but many times the very thing I have asked them about goes against Scripture, reason, and tradition. They are basing their decision to believe something and live a certain way on a supposed sign from God. This is why experience needs to be informed by the other questions.

But, after we have asked the other questions, it is also important that we ask the experience question: "Does this feel true?" Are we experiencing the fulfillment that should come from truth? Are we experiencing destruction from believing this or are we experiencing fruitfulness? We must ask the Lord in prayer to give us clarity on this question. There have been many times throughout my life where I have been faced with a big decision. After asking questions about Scripture, reason, and tradition I understood what was most likely the right thing to believe or do, but I still was not at complete peace. During those times, I have asked God to give me clarity through providing a sense of peace or a word from someone that would confirm what He was saying to me. He has been faithful to speak to me about those things when I have asked. In fact, in James 1:5 it says, "If any of you lacks wisdom, you should ask God, who gives generously to all without finding fault, and it will be given to you." This is a beautiful promise.

CONCLUSION

In this chapter, we learned that if we are to avoid apathy in the future, we must avoid the "Firewall Free Fall," or the pattern of apathy that develops from not discerning lies from truth in our daily life. We learned that good lies are hard to detect, that lies often appeal to our pride, and that lies bring destruction. We must learn to reboot discernment in our spiritual lives in order to be prepared to defend against the enemy and his lies that seek to sidetrack us. In the final chapter of this book, we will look at one last way to reboot our lives in order to prepare ourselves to avoid apathy in the future.

REFLECTION QUESTIONS

1. The beginning of this chapter talks about how we all desire limits and protection. Are you the kind of person who likes to lock all the doors and have backup plans, or are you more of a free spirit?

2. Firewall free fall is the pattern that occurs in our lives when we continue to fall back into apathy due to lies. Have you seen this pattern in your life?

3. The first principle of lies is that good lies are hard to detect. One of the ways this happens is through story. When was a time you or someone you know was deceived by a story?

4. The second principle of lies is that lies appeal to our pride. This is appropriate for our time, when our society celebrates not being under authority and the freedom of self-expression. What are some ways you have seen this principle played out in society?

5. The third principle of lies is that lies bring destruction.

What kind of destruction have you seen lies bring into your life or the lives of people around you?

6. One of the ways we can develop a spiritual firewall in our lives is to become aware. In what part of your life do you need to become most aware of lies?

7. Questions are extremely important for discernment. Are you skilled at asking questions or do you need to ask questions on a more regular basis in your life?

8. Which of the application steps below might be most difficult for you to practice? Why?

APPLICATION

1. BECOME AWARE – What is one way you can become more aware of lies in your life this week?

2. ASK MORE QUESTIONS – Sit down with a spouse, friend, or mentor this week and intentionally ask each other questions about the most important things of life.

3. WESLEYAN QUADRILATERAL – Pick a question about your life and use the Wesleyan quadrilateral (Scripture, reason, tradition, experience) to figure out an answer.

Chapter 6

Fatal Fragmentation
REBOOTING URGENCY IN OUR SPIRITUAL LIFE

Recently, I was working on a project that required me to attach glass panels to a wooden frame. A friend had given me glass panels that had pre-cut holes in the corners, so it was as simple as gently putting a screw through the corners to attach the panel to the frame. I knew the glass would be fragile and I would have to be careful as I worked with them.

I would gently lay the glass panels over the wooden frame I had built. Then very slowly I would start to tighten the screw in the corner of the panel with my drill. I would try to go straight through the holes in order to not catch the edge of the glass. But there would come this point with each panel (the point of no return you could say) where I would stop and say to myself, "It is still not quite secure, but if I push it too much further I know it is going to crack."

Sometimes, I would let it go and move on. Other times I

would say, "I could push it just a couple more turns." Several times I got away with it. But on more than one occasion I would try to gently turn the screw a couple more times and crack – the corner of the glass would splinter. Another word I could use to describe the glass would be fragmented. There was no putting it back together. In fact, if I wasn't careful that small fragmentation in the corner would spread to the rest of the panel and the whole thing would fall apart.

As we finish our study on apathy by reflecting on several ways to keep our lives from returning to apathy, I would be remiss if I did not discuss the issue of fragmentation. Merriam-Webster defines "fragment" as "a part broken off, detached, or incomplete."[75] Fragmentation then is the process by which elements of a whole start to break apart or become detached from one another.

If we know what to look for, we can see this process of fragmentation occurring in our lives on a regular basis. Just like the glass panel, we lie in a precarious position. We have been created beautiful and useful, but if pushed too far and too hard we are prone to break. We want to live a passionate life for God. Perhaps we are even living out most of the instruction in this book. Despite all of that, there are moments, seasons, and situations where the temptation to fragment can be so great.

For instance, maybe you have a young family and you are trying your best to lead your family toward godliness. You know that if you are going to do that well it will be an everyday, twenty-four hours a day job. You do all the right things by seeking God's strength instead of your own, depending on His promises, and seeking to be in His presence instead of just doing things out of obligation. This is great and will sustain you in your task. Yet, there occasionally comes a time when the difficulty of multiple kids, stressful relationships, difficult work, loneliness, and many other stressors can push so hard that it feels like things are about to crack.

Or maybe you are attempting to live a passionate life by serving people in any way you can. You are serving in your church, at the local mission, and through community organizations. You are also taking care of people in your family and seeking to invest in friendships. Since people around you rarely see so much love in action from other people, you get asked to be on every committee and to help out at every event. You may very much enjoy this and feel like you are fulfilling the kingdom of God, but there are times when you have spent so much time doing so many good things that you start to lose the point of why you are even doing it in the first place.

Now, in both examples, most of the actions being done are good and godly things. The people mentioned would be prime examples of people who are living a passionate life for Jesus. But there comes a point in our lives, like that point of no return with the glass panels, where we can push our lives too far. All the activity we are doing is good, but it is not good that we are doing so much activity. We start to lose sight of why we are even doing all the things we are doing.

When Jesus speaks to the Ephesian church in the book of Revelation, He tells them how proud He is that they have persevered and worked hard. He says in Revelation 2:2, "I know your deeds, your hard work and your perseverance." But just two verses later He says, "Yet I hold this against you: You have forsaken the love you had at first." There is a great temptation to do so many good things that we stop doing them for the right reason. We lose sight of God's vision and purpose for our life. We start assuming that all good things are

God's will for us and take on every challenge that presents itself, not realizing that with every good thing we add, our urgency for God's best starts to wane.

I call this "fatal fragmentation." For some it happens slowly, while for others it can happen as quickly as the glass breaking on my frames. It is a dividing of our lives, where things that are supposed to reside together start to break apart.

The Sacred and Secular Divide

One symptom of "fatal fragmentation" is the division of sacred and secular in our lives. When our lives are functioning under God's control and we are living a passionate life for Jesus, the dividing line between sacred and secular starts to fade away. The word "sacred' is used to describe things that are directly religious or for the purpose of honoring God. The word "secular" is used to describe things that are part of normal, everyday life and not directly religious in any way. As we become a passionate follower of Jesus, we start to recognize that all of life is sacred. As 1 Corinthians 10:31 says, "So whether you eat or drink or whatever you do, do it all for the glory of God." Meal times, bed times, traveling in the car, being at work, entertainment opportunities, and everything else we do starts to become an opportunity to glorify God. A person who views life this way no longer views church as the "religious" part of their week, and all the other time as their own. Their life is unified in vision and purpose.

If someone lives a life like this, they will start to do more and more good things aligned with this reality. People will see the passion they are living life with and will suggest many other good things for them to be a part of. If they are not careful to listen to God's direction on what good things to say "yes" to, and what things to say "no" to there may come a point where their capacity is completely overwhelmed. They start to burn out and fragment.

Before this, they would have viewed everything as an opportunity to serve the Lord, but because they feel like they are doing so much for God they start to yearn for "secular" escapes. Instead of realizing that God calls us to rest through Sabbath and relying on Him for their comfort, they start to divide their time. They start to count up their sacred "hours" and feel justified in having time where they purposely do not think about life being sacred. They start to feel like they deserve "time away from God." If this rhythm of fragmentation in their life does not stop, it can lead to even more dangerous symptoms.

The Comfort and Conflict Divide

Another symptom of "fatal fragmentation" is the tendency to avoid conflict. If we are living a passionate life for God, the dividing line between comfort and conflict starts to get thin. What I mean is that we start to embrace conflict as a natural outworking of continuing to grow with God. There will be times when we get off track, and we will need someone to come to us and tell us the truth about the situation. In fact, if we are serious about living a passionate life for God, we will seek out people who are willing to speak truth to us even if it hurts. Our only passion would be to honor God with our life and we will do that even if it hurts to hear the truth.

If we are living a passionate life for God, we also will be willing to speak the truth in love. Ephesians 4:15 explains that we must be speaking the truth in love to one another so we can all grow together to honor God. We do not walk around hypocritically looking for sin in other peoples' lives, but we are willing to speak up if we see something in another person's life that will hurt them and hurt the body of Christ.

Whether we are accepting criticism or speaking truth to another person, as a passionate follower of Jesus we become comfortable with conflict. Nineteenth century journalist Finley Peter Dunne is often remembered as saying, "The job of the newspaper is to comfort the afflicted and afflict the comfortable."[76] I believe this also defines the attitude of someone who is passionate about Jesus. We desire to live this way for others and also have others act this way toward us.

But if we start to burn out and fragment, there is a great temptation to become uncomfortable with conflict. For instance, if we start to lose our passion, it quickly becomes obvious to others around us who are passionate about God. They might not know exactly what is going on, but they will be able to tell a difference in how we are living because apathy will start to take its hold. If they truly love us like we ought to love one another, then they will lovingly confront us about it.

If "fatal fragmentation" has taken hold, then instead of being thankful that someone cares enough about us and our spiritual life to ask us about it, we might immediately react. Often, this means simply running away from the conversation and the person. If fatal fragmentation has taken its hold deeply, this may even come out in verbal slugfests, gossip, backstabbing, and all forms of anger. This angry reaction is an attempt to isolate ourselves from conflict.

I have unfortunately observed this in ministry more times than I can count. I take God's commands to love one another seriously and so when I see someone starting to slide into apathy, I try to gently ask them about it. If the "fragmentation" has not gone too deep, then they are usually thankful for my questions. But, other times, despite expressing how much I care about them and telling them that I would love to walk with them through this struggle, they simply run away.

They feel justified in running away because I have "attacked" something in their life they hold dear, not realizing that in the end this fragmentation will become destructive. One of the saddest things to me in ministry is that it sometimes takes them being at the very end of their rope and in complete distress before they come back. They are finally able to see how fragmented their life has become, but they had to walk a dark road to see it.

Now, please do not think I am just looking at others when I say this either. I have walked several roads throughout my life that have led to fragmentation. Part of the reason I can see it so easily in others now is because I have experienced those same things in my life. I have been the one that has run away and avoided conflict, feeling like I was justified, only to find out I was living a fragmented life.

Living a Life of Contradictions

A final symptom of "fatal fragmentation" is an inability to see the contradictions in our own lives. If we start to live out the sacred/secular divide and the comfort/conflict divide, there will be a great temptation to start doing things that are not godly. Remember, up until this point, we have been doing mostly good and godly things. In fact, instead of listening to what God's best is for us, we have done every good thing we can think of, which has led to burn out. But, if this burn out and fragmentation has gotten to the point where we start to isolate ourselves and divide our purpose and vision, there is a great chance that we will continue to sound godly while doing very ungodly things.

The ultimate example of this is the corrupt pastor or spiritual leader. People are left aghast at the realization that someone who is preaching and leading others in their spiritual lives could get to the point of living a life of contradictions. What they do not consider is that very few pastors started out with the intention to deceive. They started out with a passion for God and a desire to help others grow. But ministering to others can be a difficult and rocky road. If they did not take care to watch for fragmentation, before long they would start to rationalize away small sinful actions, then bigger ones. Since many pastors are taking care of others it can be easy to lose accountability themselves, and before long they may not even fully recognize the contradiction their life represents.

People can criticize spiritual leaders for this (and we do need to be held to a higher standard) while not recognizing the same contradictions can easily exist in their own lives. Fragmentation is evident when someone can easily criticize another person without seeing the exact same attitude in themselves. They have disconnected their ability to see people from God's perspective and can only see them from their human perspective.

And this is the ultimate trouble. As "fatal fragmentation" becomes more of a reality in a person's life, they lose God's perspective. If not corrected, it will lead to apathy and ultimately destruction which is why I included the word "fatal." Thankfully, although the glass that I referenced earlier could not be repaired and "fatal" is a word with finality, God's grace does allow for redemption even in the greatest of fragmentation.

DEFRAGMENTATION

What we need is defragmentation. Defragmentation or defragging is a process you can run on a computer to clean up the hard drive. As a computer works, it writes data onto the hard drive. For instance, if you save a file it has to be written to the hard drive. What the computer does, though, is to write that information wherever there is available space. The problem is if there is not enough open space on one part of the hard drive for the entire file it might physically split up the file between two or more different fragments. If this happens occasionally or for small files, it is not that big of a deal. But when it happens continually, it leads to slower performance and responsiveness from the hard drive.[77]

Defragmentation, then, is the process of bringing those fragments back into order on the hard drive. There are programs you can run to defrag the hard drive. As the program starts to patch together the different fragments on the hard drive, the computer starts to regain the performance speed it lost.

In the same way, we need a reboot of urgency in our spiritual lives to deal with fragmentation. Peter, in the final chapter of 2 Peter, deals with this very issue. He observes the results of fragmentation and then closes the letter by talking about how we should live in order to not be distracted by fragmentation.

DELIBERATELY FORGETTING

Peter has given a lot of helpful instruction to the church in the letter of 2 Peter. At the end of the letter, his intention is to remind them of what he has said thus far and to make the case for having urgency. He starts in 2 Peter 3:1 by reminding them why he wrote the letter in the first place, "Dear friends, this is now my second letter to you. I have written both of them as reminders to stimulate you to wholesome thinking." This "wholesome thinking" was a thinking "uncontaminated by the seductive influence of the senses."[78] It was not split or disjointed, but clear and able to see what God desires.

This thinking was in direct contrast with the false teachers he has talked about throughout the letter. In verse three, he calls them "scoffers." They are people who "make fun of by mocking."[79] The main issue they mock is the fact that Jesus has not returned yet. The question they are asking is "Where is this 'coming' He (Jesus) promised?"[80] This question is one of the greatest deceptions the false teachers were trying to convince people of. They were using the fact that Jesus had not returned yet as a rationalization for "following their own evil desires."[81]

How did they do this? Peter says in 2 Peter 3:5 that they "deliberately forget." Basically, "they have their own wants and pleasures, and they justify indulging those desires by raising queries about those points of theology which condemn them."[82] They "deliberately forget" God's Word which governs all things and the control and dominion He exerts over all His creation. There is nothing in this entire universe over which God does not have complete authority. In order to justify their own actions, the false teachers are deliberately forgetting God's power.

In verses 8-9, Peter next turns to God's promise. He says in 2 Peter 3:9, "The Lord is not slow in keeping his promises, as some understand slowness." The false teachers were challenging God's power because He did not seem to be acting on His promise of coming back again. So, because they denied His power, they doubted His promises. Peter warns that we must not follow their lead.

In fact, he says two interesting statements. First, he says in 2 Peter 3:8, "But do not forget this one thing, dear friends: With the Lord a day is like a thousand years, and a thousand years are like a day." What he means is, "'God sees time with a perspective we lack...[and] with an intensity we lack.' He can see the broad sweep of history in a moment, yet he can stretch out a day with patient care."[83] God's vision is much higher than ours. He can live with a focus and intensity we lack because He can see the big picture.

The other statement he says in 2 Peter 3:9b is, "Instead, he is patient with you, not wanting anyone to perish, but everyone to come to repentance." The fact that He has a vision bigger than ours allows Him to be patient. Since He knows what the ultimate outcome of all things will be, He can be patient in working out the process. His desire is for everyone to come into relationship with Him. Therefore, His patience is not a weakness, as the false teachers say, but actually a demonstration of His great power and strength.

In fact, in verse 10, Peter clearly says God's practices will demonstrate one day that His power and promises are true. There will come a day when Jesus will come back. And this time He will come as a conquering king. He will come to judge the world and to bring everything that is unjust into order. It will be a terrifying and awe-inspiring time where "the elements will be destroyed by fire, and the earth and everything done in it will be laid bare."

In the end, Peter's verdict against the scoffers is that they have deliberately forgotten God's power, promises, and practice (the very elements of apathy we have talked about in this book). In so doing, they demonstrate fatal fragmentation. They are walking contradictions, on one hand acting as though they are holier than others while on the other hand acting completely contradictory to that. Choosing to not see life from God's vantage point led them to a place of destruction in the end.

FRAGMENTED VISION

It is unlikely the false teachers started out with good intentions and fell into fatal fragmentation. It seems as though their intentions were rotten from the beginning. But, as we talked earlier in this chapter, I think very few of us intend to have fragmentation happen in our lives. In fact, I think fragmentation is most dangerous for those who are living the most passionate lives. Even if the intentions behind it are different, though, I believe the process of fragmentation happens in a similar way to the example of the false teachers.

Fatal fragmentation starts to take hold in our lives when our vision is fragmented. Vision is a term talked about incessantly in business and leadership arenas. Every conference or book focuses on the need for leaders to set a vision for their company or organization. A vision in this case is a clear idea of what the future will look like if a company starts to prioritize things the leader deems important. It allows for people and resources to be allocated in an intentional way to accomplish a particular purpose. A company or organization with a clear vision understands where they are going, why they are going there, and can easily start to design strategic means of accomplishing the vision.

One of the great things a clear vision helps a company or organization avoid is the tendency to do everything. Brian

Barrett, in an article entitled *Hey Spotify: Not every tech company needs to be everything* explains his view that too many technology companies of today are trying to do everything instead of focusing on doing some things well. He references the track record of AOL, a company that started out well but began to falter when they tried to do everything. He points out the fact that Spotify and other companies of today are following the same track in their attempt to become the one-stop shop for internet traffic. He does not think this is a good idea from a philosophical standpoint and at one point in the article says, "The more practical problem, though, is that it's unrealistic to expect any one company to be the best at any one thing, much less everything."[84]

When there is no clear vision for a company or organization, what usually follows is an attempt to do every good thing that comes along. But when there is a clear vision of what the future should look like, it allows a company or organization to say "no," even if it means saying "no" to good opportunities.

In a similar way, our lives must have a clear vision to avoid fatal fragmentation. As you have read this book, I pray you have picked up on the fact that I am not just speaking academically on the subject of apathy. I have experienced almost all the different elements of apathy in this book at some point in my life and have had to let God do much work on my heart in the process. However, if I could point to the one chapter that has been the greatest area of personal struggle, it would probably be this chapter.

I have always been the person who did not want to miss out on anything. When I was a little kid, if my parents had company visiting, I would hate being put to bed. I was afraid I would miss out on an interesting conversation or fun experience. I would sneak out of my room and sit at the top of the stairs sometimes just to see if I could hear what they were talking about.

As I got older, I was always "all in" to whatever I was doing at the time. If it was school, I would hate to miss out on any opportunities there and always chose to challenge myself. If it was some kind of musical opportunity, I would try to do it all and be a part of every group I had access to. If it was something at church, I wanted to be there the whole time and not miss a thing. Socially, academically, spiritually...I wanted to do it all.

Nothing I wanted to do was bad. In fact, most of the things were really good. I wanted to be a great student, I wanted to be a great musician, I wanted to serve God well and do ministry, I wanted to be a good son and friend, etc. The problem is I had failed to learn this important lesson: it is not my job to do *every* good thing that comes my way, and if I try to do everything I will lose sight of God's best for me.

Fatal fragmentation always came into my life when things got most stressful. I could always handle a large amount of stress, so I had to be pushed to my very limits to feel it sometimes. In high school, there was a period in which I was involved in ten different music groups, several clubs, many church ministries, and AP classes at school, all while not forgetting my friendships and family. In several of those groups I was in leadership and had extra responsibilities. Now, from a human standpoint I could handle it. It was all fun and enjoyable to me. I was good at most of it, and I could rationalize why each one of those things was an opportunity for me to live for God. But if I would have been watching correctly, I could have observed fragmentation starting to occur.

In college, it got severely worse. At one point, I was taking thirteen classes per semester and had four majors. I was in the honors college at the school and participated in several music groups which took occasional long-distance trips. At the same time, I was also doing dorm ministry, trying to have a social life, trying to prepare for a life of pastoral ministry, and trying to sleep a little bit. Again, I could rationalize the value of any one of these different activities; they were all good things.

The problem at both of these stages of life was that I started to get fragmented vision. Because I was doing everything, I was not doing anything well. I stopped asking why I was doing what I was doing. I stopped truly asking what the best things God wanted me to do were, and instead I was ultimately doing what I thought was best.

As a result of this fragmented vision I started to burn out. All the symptoms of fragmentation started to become evident in my life. I started to want "a break" from the sacred, I tried to avoid conflict, and even if my life was not an overt contradiction, I knew deep down I was not living out what I was preaching. Even though I would preach about a passionate life with Jesus, my own relationship with Him felt empty.

The reason this fragmented vision ultimately occurred is because I forgot the ultimate goal and aim of my life. Just as Peter details in 2 Peter 3 how the false teachers "deliberately forget" God's power, promises, and practices in order to do what they want, we can start to "deliberately forget" the ultimate goal of our life.

Brother Lawrence, in *The Practice of the Presence of God* says this about our lives: "Let us think often that our only business in this life is to please God. Perhaps all besides is but folly and vanity."[85] Don't we overcomplicate life sometimes? Our lives are simply supposed to be pleasing to God. There are no other goals or aims. There are no other mission statements or visionary plans that should overshadow the simplicity of this statement. We are simply called to please God. When we are doing this, we will be whole and not divided. We will be in the center of God's will. We will not always be comfortable, but we will be satisfied.

What Causes Fragmented Vision?

When our vision starts to fragment, it does so for one of several reasons. Maybe, like the false teachers, we desire something different than pleasing God. We want to do what we want to do. This could even be good things. These kinds of situations happen all the time with parents and kids. On one recent night, we were visiting my parents and it was time to get my son Judah home to sleep. I asked him to get his coat and shoes on so we could go. He tried many different ways to keep playing with his toys or doing something else to avoid leaving. He did not want to go to bed.

We have been trying to teach him, even as young as he is, that God desires obedience from us because He loves us and He knows that what He requires will be the best in the end. And we always try to reinforce that this is why God asks children to honor and obey their parents. As parents, the big picture is clear to us. If he decided to play (which in and of itself is not a bad thing) all night, we know he would have a terrible day the next day, would be more open to illness, and would ultimately not have fun playing with his toys the next day. All our son sees is that there is nothing wrong with playing toys and he does not know why we want to hold him back from playing with them. In the same way, vision may start to fragment in your life because you want to do something that at face value is not necessarily a bad thing, but you know it is not God's best.

I only had one other long-term relationship before my wife. I dated a couple of other girls over the years, but nothing too serious. Toward the end of college, though, I met this girl who was a chaplain in one of the dorms. I was one of the student body chaplains at the time and we got to know each other through that connection. We started dating during my senior year of college. After college, I had moved back with my parents for a time and her family did not live far from where my parents lived. We kept the relationship going while I was working in the area where my parents lived.

She was a nice girl who was really trying to live like Jesus. We were trying to honor God with the relationship and there was no sense of impropriety in it. Yet, during that season of the relationship, I started to sense it was not what God wanted for me. It got to the point where one day, as I was reading my Bible, I had the closest thing I have ever had to a "vision" where several verses from one page of Scripture seemed to jump off the page at me. All the verses directly connected with the fact that I needed to break off the relationship.

I quickly closed my Bible and sat there a little stunned. I could have immediately responded to what God was saying to me even though it might have been difficult. Instead, partially because of the fear of not having someone in my life, the fragmentation started to happen. I started to rationalize away why God would say this to me. I would express to myself how we had stayed pure in the relationship. I would remind myself how she was a nice, godly girl. I would even try to rationalize away how this "vision" was probably not God. But deep down

I knew it was God speaking to me. I began to "deliberately forget" and continued in the relationship even though it was not what God wanted.

Some time passed and I ended up moving to Buffalo, New York. We continued the relationship long distance during that time, but I could feel myself fragmenting, becoming less and less authentic and passionate. I was expending so much energy on rationalizing away what I was doing that I had no energy to give to being authentically on fire for God. It started to wear away at my love for God and my love for this girl. Looking back, through this experience, I could see how easily a marriage could start to break apart if one or both spouses decided to not defend against fragmentation.

Finally, I could not take it anymore. During Christmas break I invited my girlfriend to fly up to Buffalo and visit. She stayed where my parents were living at the time. I did not invite her there to break up with her. In fact, I was still doing everything I could to make it work. But the fragmentation had hit the breaking point. One day, I took her out to Niagara Falls and I was in such torment about the whole situation that I did not talk very much. I was silent in the car on the way back. Finally, knowing I could not do this anymore, I pulled the car over into a Tim Horton's coffee shop parking lot and broke up with her.

I felt a relief about finally listening to the Lord, but I realized how much more pain I caused my girlfriend by waiting so long to listen to God. In fact, one thing I did not factor into this situation was that her flight home did not leave for a couple days and she could not get a different one. So, when I took her back to my parent's place, they were not surprised I broken up with her, but were shocked that I had chosen that moment. Now the poor girl had to stay in a house with her ex-boyfriend's family for a couple days. Needless to say, I felt bad for how awkward it was for her. God ultimately brought healing in both of our lives and the timing of this break-up became a neat connection in the story of my wife and I getting together, but this is an example of how destructive it can be to follow our own fragmented vision instead of God's.

Another reason we can have fragmented vision is not necessarily because we do not want to please God, but because we do not know what He wants. We do everything that seems right to do because we think it is what God desires, without realizing that not everything we are doing is God's best. We may start very passionately and urgently at this endeavor, but the more things we try to tackle, the less passionate and urgent we become. Peter begins in verse 3:11 to describe what rebooting the urgency of our spiritual life looks like.

Rebooting Urgency in our Spiritual Life

Peter says in 2 Peter 3:11, "Since everything will be destroyed in this way, what kind of people ought you to be? You ought to live holy and godly lives as you look forward to the day of God and speed its coming." Just before this in verse 10, he has been talking about the fact that the "day of the Lord will come like a thief." What he means is that Jesus could come back at any time; we do not know when this will be. If His return could happen at any time, then how should this change the way we live?

Jesus tells a series of parables regarding His return in Matthew 24 and 25. In Matthew 24:36 it says, "But about that day or hour no one knows, not even the angels in heaven, nor the Son, but only the Father." He then goes on to use parables to talk about how fragmented our living can become when we choose to distance ourselves from the reality of Jesus' eventual return.

First, in Matthew 24:45, He speaks of a "faithful and wise servant, whom the master has put in charge of the servants in his household to give them their food at the proper time." He says the master will return at some point and it will be good if the master sees him doing what he was asked to do. He will be rewarded for following the master's instructions.

But then He speaks of the wicked servant. He says in verses 48-49, "But suppose that servant is wicked and says to himself, 'My master is staying away a long time and he then begins to beat his fellow servants and to eat and drink with drunkards." Jesus says this servant will be caught off guard when his master returns and will suffer judgment.

The next parable Jesus tells is the parable of the ten virgins. There were five wise virgins and five foolish ones. The bridegroom, who represents Jesus, is delayed in getting there for the procession they were to walk in. The wise ones were prepared to meet with the bridegroom with their lamps full of oil. The foolish ones were not prepared with enough oil. When the bridegroom arrives at midnight, the foolish virgins are forced to go find oil somewhere else and they miss the procession, while the wise virgins "who were ready went in with him to the wedding banquet."[86] The wedding banquet represents the wedding feast of the Lamb where all those who have followed Jesus will be present in the end.

In a third parable, Jesus says His return will be like a man who is going on a journey, but before he leaves, he entrusts a bag of gold to three different servants. To one he gives five bags of gold, to another he gives two bags, and still another he gives one bag. The first two servants went and put that money to work and doubled the bags of gold they were given. The third servant took his one bag of money and hid it in the ground.

When the master returns, he is pleased that the first two servants kept their master's return in mind and were intentional to double his investment in them. He says to both of them, "Well done, good and faithful servant! You have been faithful with a few things; I will put you in charge of many things. Come and share your master's happiness!"[87] The third servant tries to rationalize why he buried the money, but the master is not pleased. The master calls him a "wicked, lazy servant" and tells him that if nothing else he should have given the money to bankers so at least it would have accrued interest.[88]

The point of all three parables is simple. Whether the people in the parables decided to do wicked things or were unprepared or chose to waste the time and resources they were given, they all lost sight of the master's return. Their actions became fragmented and disjointed because they did not keep the end in mind. A quote I use often that reflects this reality is a statement by C.S. Lewis in his book *Mere Christianity*:

> *If you read history you will find that the Christians who did most for the present world were just those who thought most of the next. The Apostles themselves, who set on foot the conversion of the Roman Empire, the great men who built up the Middle Ages, the English Evangelicals who abolished the Slave Trade, all left their mark on Earth, precisely because their minds were occupied with Heaven. It is since Christians have largely ceased to think of the other world that they have become so ineffective in this. Aim at Heaven and you will get earth "thrown in": aim at earth and you will get neither.*[89]

If we forget heaven and the return of Jesus, we will invariably start to lead a fragmented life. We will say, "I know

Jesus is coming back someday, but it seems so far away and intangible. In the meantime, God won't mind if I do things my way for a little bit. I mean, He'll forgive me in the end anyway." But nobody is satisfied with fragmented living. At first, we might think it will give us more freedom, but in the end, we will never be truly satisfied. Only when we have a completely God-centered focus and vision on our ultimate destiny will we have clarity on how to live in the present.

So, the primary way we reboot urgency in our spiritual lives is to keep our minds focused on the ultimate goal of heaven. It has become popular in church circles in this generation to downplay heaven. Part of the reason this has occurred is because there is a younger generation of believers that grew up hearing great evangelists and speakers talk about getting a ticket to heaven while giving the impression that it was not important to care for the needs of the world now. As a reaction, many younger Christian leaders have given the impression that thinking about heaven is not all that important. Instead, they encourage people to simply dream about making a difference in the world now.

The problem with this is when we stop dreaming about heaven, we start forgetting about what is most important. Our vision becomes fragmented; doing all kinds of really good things, but missing out on God's best. All of a sudden, many of the actions we are taking do not look like someone who is ready for heaven. This is dangerous not only for us, but also for those we are influencing.

When we choose to keep our minds focused on heaven, it first reminds us of the need to live lives that demonstrate God's grace to others. Earlier, we discussed how fragmentation leads to a life of contradictions. This does nothing to prepare ourselves or other people for heaven. In contrast, Peter says in

2 Peter 3:14, "So then, dear friends, since you are looking forward to this, make every effort to be found spotless, blameless, and at peace with him." This immediately confronts the contradictions in our lives and leads us to ask God the question, "What is Your will for my life?" It is such a simple question, but one that will keep you from living a fragmented life.

So often we pray to God about things we need or things others need. But, I find most of us rarely take enough time when we pray to ask God questions. It is almost as if we think God is there if we need him to help us with something, but we have to come up with the plan. Instead, God is ready and willing to tell us what He wants for our lives if we simply ask. If you are in a situation where there are many good opportunities available to you and you do not know the best way to go, simply ask Him. When we are willing to be in the center of God's will at all times, we can live "at peace with Him." When people see us living at peace with God, it will point them to the place where true peace can be found.

The other thing that happens when we keep our minds focused on heaven is it heightens our awareness of people's eternal destiny. Peter says in 2 Peter 3:15, "Bear in mind that our Lord's patience means salvation, just as our dear brother also wrote you with the wisdom that God gave him." God is patiently waiting, but He will one day come to judge the world. Do the actions of our lives align with the fact that today or tomorrow Jesus could come back? Are the good things we are doing actually leading to people knowing Jesus more?

I remember reading a book years ago by a Christian leader who related a story about ministering to someone who had AIDS. This Christian leader would have been from this segment of the church that downplays a focus on heaven in order to focus more attention on current needs on earth. The person sat with the AIDS patient and comforted him. He did not want to be pushy about heaven and just wanted to care for his immediate needs. At the end of the story, the man with AIDS died beside the Christian leader and he relates in the book how much he learned from watching that struggle.

Unless I missed something, I was a little shaken by the story. I admired this person's sensitivity and care for the needs of a man with a terrible disease. We should be doing things like that as Christians. But to my understanding this Christian leader never overtly shared the Gospel with the man who was dying. I was shocked by the fact that although he was trying to do all kinds of good things, he lost sight of heaven. If we believe what the Scriptures say, then each one of us has an eternal destiny, either in heaven or in hell. When we remember there is an eternal destiny ahead for every person on this planet, it can help to reboot the urgency of our spiritual life.

HOW TO DO IT?

These last couple chapters have talked about how to prepare our lives so we do not fall back into apathy in the future. Fatal fragmentation is often a difficult thing to discern in our own lives because it usually happens over a long period of time and can come in the midst of doing great things. It is very similar to a hard drive that needs defragmenting, like we talked about earlier in the chapter. A hard drive gets fragmented simply by information being spread out too far in the normal process of saving information. But a hard drive cannot defragment itself. It needs to submit to the power of a defragmentation program. The program simply reorders the hard drive so that all the different parts of files are in the proper location again. Divided information and data comes back together and gets reordered. It is suggested that a person runs this program on a semi-regular basis on their hard drive in order to keep it performing well.

In a similar way, in order to avoid fatal fragmentation, it is so important to occasionally submit the "hard drive" of your life to the Lord for defragmenting. Sometimes, you will sense fragmentation happening in your soul and know you need to do this as soon as possible.

I have also found a good time to do this is at a natural break in activity. For instance, at the start of a new year or the end of a semester of school or on a vacation from work or on a break from the ministry you are volunteering in. In these natural breaks, it is a good practice (even if there is nothing that seems fragmented in your life) to bring your schedule and all of your activities before the Lord and ask Him what He thinks.

I find in these times it is usually good to recount the reason why I exist and the importance of remembering heaven before I spend time looking over the state of life. You might bring your calendar, a list of what you have accomplished in the past year, a copy of your bank account statement, and a journal and simply ask God to give you wisdom as you look through it. You might find it helpful to ask questions such as:

- Does everything on my calendar please God and serve the mission of helping others know about Jesus?
- Do the accomplishments from my past year demonstrate an urgency about loving God and loving others?
- Do my finances/time line up with a clear vision of

heaven?

- Where do I see fragmentation happening in my life and why is it happening?

As you ask these questions, it is important to listen to the voice of God. How would He re-order things in your life to make you the most effective for His Kingdom?

Then, after evaluating the past year or segment of time, it is important to turn your attention to the future and ask God what He wants for that. It might be helpful to ask questions like this:

- What are some things God wants me to say "yes" to and what are some things that God wants me to say "no" to?
- How does God want the rhythm of my schedule and my family's schedule to look?
- What are some intentional ways I can use the resources I have been given to share the Gospel with others?

After you have put together the answers to these questions and feel confident it is what God wants for you, it is wise to share this with someone close to you whether that is a friend, family member, or pastor. They can give you feedback and watch for any signs of fragmentation as you continue forward, living a passionate life for Jesus.

I especially encourage families to do this together and hold each other accountable in the process. When I was leading a college ministry for many years, I cannot tell you how many times I heard from parents that watched their high school or college-aged kids walk away from a relationship with

God. Often, the parents were dumbfounded because they had brought the kids to church their whole life and tried to teach them about Jesus.

As I would observe and ask questions, though, it became obvious that one of the greatest reasons most of the kids were walking away from God was because of fatal fragmentation. The parents would know that teaching their kids to follow God was important, but they never helped their children see that in order to become a passionate follower of God they had to offer everything they have to the Lord, even their schedule. So, I would watch as parents of middle schoolers and high schoolers had their student doing every academic, sports, and musical activity you could think of. Every night of their schedule was jam packed with all kinds of good things.

Often this meant that church and a relationship with Jesus became another thing on the to-do list instead of the one main unifying purpose of life. Learning to spend time with Jesus personally was not on the radar because they were too busy with all the other aspects of life. Free time to spend thinking, reflecting, and investing in relationships was jettisoned in favor of constant activity.

It broke my heart to watch this happen over and over again. By the time these students got to college and were challenged, a relationship with God was no more than a small piece of their life at that point. This fragmentation could have been avoided if those families had simply sat together growing up and demonstrated how to set up life doing only God's best and not everything. Sometimes, it means sacrificing good things in order to gain God's best.

CONCLUSION

In this chapter, we learned that if we are to avoid apathy in the future, we must avoid the "Fatal Fragmentation," or the process by which we fill our lives with so many good things, but not God's best for us. We learned that fragmentation happens when our vision of the ultimate purpose of life gets crowded out by other activity. We must learn to reboot urgency in our spiritual lives by submitting our schedules and other elements of our life to God to ensure we are focusing our attention on His best for us.

REFLECTION QUESTIONS

1. What comes to mind when you think of the word "fragmented?" Do you ever feel like it could be applied to your life?

2. Have you ever seen a sacred and secular divide start to grow in your life? What did it look like when that happened?

3. Have you ever noticed a comfort and conflict divide start to happen in your life? Why do you think it is such a temptation to run away from conflict?

4. Why is it so hard to acknowledge when we have started to live a life of contradictions?

5. When we start to get fragmented vision about what life is about it leads us to fatal fragmentation. Do you have a clear vision about what your life should look like in this season? If not, why not?

6. It is so important that we remember heaven if we are to keep our lives from becoming fragmented. How often do you think about heaven? Why do you think it is easy to forget heaven in our daily life?

7. Which of the application steps below might be most difficult for you to practice? Why?

APPLICATION

1. KEEP YOUR MIND FOCUSED – One of the greatest ways to avoid fatal fragmentation is to keep your mind focused on your ultimate goal. What are some actions you can take to keep your mind focused on heaven?
2. DEFRAGMENTATION – Take time to sit down and go through the questions toward the end of the chapter.
3. FAMILY MEETING – If you have a family, sit down and go through your calendar together. Take time to ask the Lord if your family calendar is keeping the most important things in mind.

CONCLUSION

Have you ever opened a brand-new computer or piece of technology? There is something exciting about it. There is the bright shiny packaging, that clean metallic smell, and the shiny new gloss of the machine. Some people skip the instructions and go straight to the computer, but I tend to look at the instructions first to make sure I use it properly. Then, after I skim my way through the instructions I push the power button for the first time. Light flashes across the screen. There is great excitement for how each new feature of this piece of technology works.

After you have used it for a while, though, there is no longer the same kind of excitement. Pushing the power button just becomes the thing you have to do every day. The bright screen starts to fade over time from dust and dirt. This piece of technology has withstood spilled drinks, being carried in a crowded bag, a couple falls, and years upon years of use. You may start using the technology because you have to, not because you want to. If you could replace it you would, but you know it would cost a lot.

As the machine gets older and older, it may start to fail more often than it used to. You have to look back at the set of instructions you set aside when you first opened it in order to diagnose the problems you are seeing. It might even get to the point that if you do not take significant action the computer may fail, never to start again.

I have written this book to be a sort of instruction guide to the spiritual life. Just like an instruction guide is helpful in setting up a computer or diagnosing technology problems, my prayer is that this book has met you where you are. If you are new in your faith and just getting started, I hope it has given you some clarity on how to set up your life to be passionate about Jesus for the rest of your life. If you have been a Christian for a little while and you feel as though you are just going through the motions, my hope is that you have been able to diagnose some of the reasons why you have become apathetic. And if you have gotten to the point where things are so messed up that you are not sure about faith in Jesus anymore, I hope you have found some hope in this book clarifying that Jesus is the answer.

But like all instructions books, there comes a point where you have to stop reading and you have to take action. Peter ends his letter this way in 2 Peter 3:17-18:

Therefore, dear friends, since you have been forewarned, be on your guard so that you may not be carried away by the error of the lawless and fall from your secure position. But grow in the grace and knowledge of our Lord and Savior Jesus Christ. To him be glory both now and forever! Amen.

His encouragement after all his instruction to the church is to take action by growing "in the grace and knowledge of our Lord and Savior Jesus Christ." It is no small task. It is a task that is hard to measure and never ends. It is less about earning some recognition or standing and more about becoming someone through Jesus.

Throughout the process of writing this book, my primary concern was that people might quickly lose interest because it is not a flashy topic. Discipleship and the transforming work of Jesus is difficult and hard. It takes all that we are. But I pray it has become clear throughout the book the enormous blessing that comes with being a passionate follower of Jesus. Being at peace with God is the true satisfaction we all seek.

So as we come to the end, I encourage you to take up the responsibility we have to keep growing with the Lord every day. New challenges await. Life does not stand still and neither do we. As Lucas and Green say about Peter's instruction to the believers of the time, "It is as though he is saying that it is impossible to stand still as a Christian, for we all have an in-built tendency to push Jesus Christ to the back of our minds. The only remedy is to make deliberate, constant, and frequent efforts to bring him to the front."[90]

As we grow, our constant goal every day should be "to come into a deeper consciousness of Christ's love and favor."[91] As we allow God to reboot every part of our lives (our power, promises, practices, memory, discernment, and urgency) we will discover the life we have always wanted and desired. We will discover there are depths to His love we never knew existed. And even if the world around us becomes more complicated, we will realize how simple a passionate life for Jesus Christ can be. Life will become about Jesus from our first waking moment to the last moment before our eyes close. He will be our one true focus and our only aim.

May we take up the challenge to reboot, no matter the cost, and watch as He changes our lives, our families, and the world!

1 "Apathy," Dictionary.com, accessed January 4, 2018, https://www.dictionary.com/browse/apathy.

2 John 10:10 NIV

3 Acts 4:32 NIV

4 Donald W. Burdick and John H. Skilton, "2 Peter Introduction," in *NIV Study Bible* (Grand Rapids, Michigan: Zondervan, 2008), p. 1934.

5 "Reboot," Merriam-Webster Dictionary, accessed January 4, 2018, https://www.merriam-webster.com/dictionary/reboot.

6 "Hardware," Oxford Living Dictionaries, accessed January 4, 2018, https://en.oxforddictionaries.com/definition/hardware.

7 "Software," Business Dictionary, accessed January 4, 2018, http://www.businessdictionary.com/definition/software.html.

8 "Energy from Matter," Nobelprize.org, Nobel Media AB, accessed January 4, 2018, http://www.nobelprize.org/educational/physics/energy/fusion_2.html.

9 Jay Bennett, "Here's How Much Deadlier Today's Nukes are Compared to WWII A-Bombs," Popular Mechanics, October 10, 2016, accessed on January 4, 2018, http://www.popularmechanics.com/military/a23306/nuclear-bombs-powerful-today/.

10 Michael Green, "2 Peter and Jude: And Introduction and Commentary," in *Tyndale Commentary*, ed. Leon Morris (Illinois:

Intervarsity Press, 1987), 70.

[11] Dick Lucas and Christopher Green, "The Message of 2 Peter and Jude," in *The Bible Speaks Today*, ed. John R.W. Stott (Illinois: Intervaristy Press, 1995), 45.

[12] Elmer G. Homrighausen, "The Second Epistle of Peter," in *The Interpreter's Bible*, ed. George Arthur Buttrick (Tennessee: Abingdon Press, 1957), 172.

[13] Lucas and Green, "The Message of 2 Peter and Jude," in *The Bible Speaks Today*, 48.

[14] Lucas and Green, "The Message of 2 Peter and Jude," in *The Bible Speaks Today*, 21.

[15] Lucas and Green, "The Message of 2 Peter and Jude," in *The Bible Speaks Today*, 37.

[16] "Morpheus Quotable Quote," Goodreads, accessed January 4, 2018, https://www.goodreads.com/quotes/1158642-this-is-your-last-chance-after-this-there-is-no.

[17] Iain S. Maclean, "Confession," in *Eerdman's Dictionary of the Bible*, ed. David Noel Freedman (Wm. B. Eerdman's Publishing Co, 2000), 274.

[18] Romans 4:17 NIV

[19] Margaret Rouse, "Operating System (OS)," Whatis.com, TechTarget, September 2016, accessed on January 4, 2018, http://whatis.techtarget.com/definition/operating-system-OS.

[20] Tim Bower, "1.6 Parts of an Operating System," K-State Polytechnic, accessed on January 4, 2018, http://faculty.salina.k-state.edu/tim/ossg/Introduction/parts.html.

[21] Jeremiah 17:9 ESV

[22] Justin Jones, *Engage: How to Know God*, February 2017.

[23] Elmer G. Homrighausen, "The Second Epistle of Peter," in *The Interpreter's Bible*, 173.

[24] Steven B. Cowan, "Covenant," in *Holman Illustrated Bible Dictionary* (Nashville, Tennessee: Holman Bible Publishers, 2003).

[25] Michael Green, "2 Peter and Jude: And Introduction and Commentary," in *Tyndale Commentary*, 83.

[26] Ephesians 2:4-5 NIV

[27] Timothy P. Jenney, "Sanctification," in *Eerdman's Dictionary of the Bible*, ed. David Noel Freedman (Wm. B. Eerdman's Publishing Co, 2000), 1165.

[28] Hebrews 13:5 NIV

[29] "Root Definition," The Linux Information Project, October 27, 2007, accessed January 4, 2018, http://www.linfo.org/root.html.

[30] Ibid.

[31] Lucas and Green, "The Message of 2 Peter and Jude," in *The Bible Speaks Today*, 63.

[32] Michael Green, "2 Peter and Jude: And Introduction and Commentary," in *Tyndale Commentary*, 86.

[33] Lucas and Green, "The Message of 2 Peter and Jude," in *The Bible Speaks Today*, 57.

[34] Ibid.

[35] Michael Green, "2 Peter and Jude: And Introduction and Commentary," in *Tyndale Commentary*, 87.

[36] "Emulation," TechTerms, June 26, 2008, accessed on January 5, 2018, https://techterms.com/definition/emulation.

[37] Lucas and Green, "The Message of 2 Peter and Jude," in *The Bible Speaks Today*, 59.

[38] Erin El Issa, "2017 American Household Credit Card Debt Survey," Nerdwallet, accessed January 5, 2018, https://www.nerdwallet.com/blog/average-credit-card-debt-household/.

[39] Lucas and Green, "The Message of 2 Peter and Jude," in *The Bible Speaks Today*, 60.

[40] Lucas and Green, "The Message of 2 Peter and Jude," in *The Bible Speaks Today*, 61.

[41] "Volatility," Merriam-Webster Dictionary, accessed January

6, 2018, https://www.merriam-webster.com/dictionary/volatility.

[42] "Computer – Memory," Tutorialspoint, accessed January 6, 2018, https://www.tutorialspoint.com/computer_fundamentals/computer_memory.htm

[43] "Memory," Computer Hope, December 29, 2017, accessed January 6, 2018, https://www.computerhope.com/jargon/m/memory.htm.

[44] Lucas and Green, "The Message of 2 Peter and Jude," in *The Bible Speaks Today*, 68.

[45] Matthew 26:35 NIV

[46] Lucas and Green, "The Message of 2 Peter and Jude," in *The Bible Speaks Today*, 68.

[47] Chris Kirby, "What happens when my computer runs out of memory (RAM)?" The Computer Group, May 19, 2011, accessed January 6, 2018, http://www.thecomputergroup.com/blog/what-happens-when-my-computer-runs-out-of-memory-ram.

[48] Elmer G. Homrighausen, "The Second Epistle of Peter," in *The Interpreter's Bible*, 179.

[49] Elmer G. Homrighausen, "The Second Epistle of Peter," in *The Interpreter's Bible*, 182.

[50] Michael Green, "2 Peter and Jude: And Introduction and

Commentary," in *Tyndale Commentary*, 111.

51 Bill Gaultiere, "Chew your Cud on God's Word," Soul
Shepherding, August 11, 2005, accessed January 7, 2018,
http://www.soulshepherding.org/2005/08/chew-your-cud-
on-gods-word/.

52 "What is a firewall?" Microsoft, accessed January 7, 2018,
https://www.microsoft.com/en-us/safety/pc-
security/firewalls-whatis.aspx.

53 Lucas and Green, "The Message of 2 Peter and Jude," in *The
Bible Speaks Today*, 68.

54 2 Peter 2:1 NIV

55 Lucas and Green, "The Message of 2 Peter and Jude," in *The
Bible Speaks Today*, 87.

56 Anthony K. Tjan, "The Indispensible Power of Story,"
Harvard Business Review, April 15, 2014, accessed January 7,
2018, https://hbr.org/2014/04/the-indispensable-power-of-
story.

57 Margaret Rouse, Mike Cobb, and Peter Loshin, "Phishing,"
Whatis.com, TechTarget, October 2017, accessed on January 7,
2018, http://whatis.techtarget.com/definition/operating-
system-OS.

58 Laura Egolf, "11 Quotes from the Screwtape Letters that
Make it So Worth Reading," Odyssey, June 27, 2016, accessed
January 7, 2018, https://www.theodysseyonline.com/musing-

screwtape-letters.

59 Ibid.

60 Ibid.

61 Lucas and Green, "The Message of 2 Peter and Jude," in *The Bible Speaks Today*, 89.

62 Lucas and Green, "The Message of 2 Peter and Jude," in *The Bible Speaks Today*, 119.

63 Katherine Timpf, "16 Most Ridiculously PC Moments on College Campuses in 2016," National Review, December 30, 2016, accessed January 7, 2018, http://www.nationalreview.com/article/443429/16-most-ridiculously-pc-moments-college-campuses-2016.

64 Ibid.

65 2 Peter 2:17 NIV

66 2 Peter 2:18 NIV

67 Lucas and Green, "The Message of 2 Peter and Jude," in *The Bible Speaks Today*, 116.

68 John 4:14 NIV

69 2 Peter 2:17 NIV

70 Lucas and Green, "The Message of 2 Peter and Jude," in *The Bible Speaks Today*, 118.

[71] Lucas and Green, "The Message of 2 Peter and Jude," in *The Bible Speaks Today*, 118-119.

[72] Elmer G. Homrighausen, "The Second Epistle of Peter," in *The Interpreter's Bible*, 190.

[73] Elmer G. Homrighausen, "The Second Epistle of Peter," in *The Interpreter's Bible*, 187.

[74] John MacArthur, "What is biblical discernment and why is it important?" Grace to You, accessed January 7, 2018, https://www.gty.org/library/questions/QA138/what-is-biblical-discernment-and-why-is-it-important.

[75] "Fragment," Merriam-Webster Dictionary, accessed January 7, 2018, https://www.merriam-webster.com/dictionary/fragment.

[76] David Shedden, "Today in Media History: Mr. Dooley: 'The job of the newspaper is to comfort the afflicted and afflict the comfortable,'" Poynter, October 7, 2014, accessed January 7, 2018, https://www.poynter.org/news/today-media-history-mr-dooley-job-newspaper-comfort-afflicted-and-afflict-comfortable.

[77] Tim Fisher, "What is fragmentation and defragmentation," Lifewire, April 6, 2017, accessed January 7, 2018, https://www.lifewire.com/what-is-fragmentation-defragmentation-2625884.

[78] Michael Green, "2 Peter and Jude: And Introduction and Commentary," in *Tyndale Commentary*, 145.

[79] Johannes P. Louw and Eugene A. Nida, *Greek-English Lexicon of the New Testament Based on Semantic Domains* (New York, NY: The United Bible Societies, 1989).

[80] 2 Peter 3:4 NIV

[81] 2 Peter 3:3 NIV

[82] Lucas and Green, "The Message of 2 Peter and Jude," in *The Bible Speaks Today*, 129.

[83] Lucas and Green, "The Message of 2 Peter and Jude," in *The Bible Speaks Today*, 137.

[84] Brian Barrett, "Hey Spotify: Not every Tech Company needs to be Everything," Wired, May 21, 2015, accessed January 7, 2018, https://www.wired.com/2015/05/hey-spotify-not-every-tech-company-needs-everything/.

[85] Brother Lawrence, *The Practice of the Presence of God*, ed. Lightheart (Project Gutenberg, 2001), http://thepracticeofthepresenceofgod.com/onlinetext/

[86] Matthew 25:10b

[87] Matthew 25:21, 23 NIV

[88] Matthew 25:26 NIV

[89] C.S. Lewis, *Mere Christianity* (1952; San Francisco: HarperSanFrancisco, 2001).

[90] Lucas and Green, "The Message of 2 Peter and Jude," in *The Bible Speaks Today*, 156.

[91] Elmer G. Homrighausen, "The Second Epistle of Peter," in *The Interpreter's Bible*, 200.

Made in the USA
Middletown, DE
05 April 2022

63620371R00106